THE AMITABHA SUTRA AS DISCOURSED BY THE BUDDHA

佛說阿彌陀經

Fo Guang Shan International Translation Center

Published by Fo Guang Shan International Translation Center
3456 Glenmark Drive
Hacienda Heights, CA 91745 U.S.A.
Tel: (626) 330-8361 / (626) 330-8362
Fax: (626) 330-8363
www.fgsitc.org

Printed in Taiwan.

THE AMITABHA SUTRA AS DISCOURSED BY THE BUDDHA

佛說阿彌陀經

目　錄

Table of Contents

Lu Xiang Zan

爐 香 讚

Lu	Xiang	Zha	Ruo			
爐	香	乍	爇			
Fa	Jie	Meng	Xun			
法	界	蒙	薰			
Zhu	Fo	Hai	Hui	Xi	Yao	Wen
諸	佛	海	會	悉	遙	聞
Sui	Chu	Jie	Xiang	Yun		
隨	處	結	祥	雲		
Cheng	Yi	Fang	Yin			
誠	意	方	殷			
Zhu	Fo	Xian	Quan	Shen		
諸	佛	現	全	身		
Nan	Mo	Xiang	Yun	Gai	Pu	Sa
南	無	香	雲	蓋	菩	薩
Mo	He	Sa				
摩	訶	薩	（三稱三拜）			

Praise of Incense Offering

Incense burning in the censer,

All space permeated with fragrance.

Buddhas perceive it from every direction.

Auspicious clouds gather everywhere.

With our sincerity,

Buddhas manifest themselves in their entirety.

We take refuge in the bodhisattvas, mahasattvas.

(repeat three times and prostrations)

Nan Mo Lian Chi Hai Hui Fo Pu Sa
南 無 蓮 池 海 會 佛 菩 薩 (三稱)

Fo Shuo O Mi Tuo Jing
佛 說 阿 彌 陀 經

Ru Shi Wo Wen
如 是 我 聞：

Yi Shi Fo Zai She Wei Guo Qi
一 時， 佛 在 舍 衛 國 祇

Shu Ji Gu Du Yuan Yu Da Bi
樹 給 孤 獨 園， 與 大 比

Qiu Seng Qian Er Bai Wu Shi Ren
丘 僧 千 二 百 五 十 人

Ju Jie Shi Da O Luo Han Zhong
俱， 皆 是 大 阿 羅 漢， 眾

We take refuge in the Buddhas and bodhisattvas of the Lotus Pond Great Assembly.

(repeat three times)

The Amitabha Sutra as Discoursed by the Buddha

Thus have I heard:

Once the Buddha was staying at Jetavana, Anathapindika's Park in the Kingdom of Sravasti with a great sangha of *bhiksus*,[1] one thousand two hundred and fifty in all. All were great arhats who the multitudes knew and recognized, [...]

1. A male member of the Buddhist monastic community who has renounced the household life and received full ordination.

Suo	Zhi	Shi	Zhang	Lao	She	Li	Fo
所	知	識。	長	老	舍	利	弗、
Mo	He	Mu	Jian	Lian	Mo	He	Jia
摩	訶	目	犍	連、	摩	訶	迦
She	Mo	He	Jia	Zhan	Yan	Mo	He
葉、	摩	訶	迦	旃	延、	摩	訶
Ju	Chi	Luo	Li	Po	Duo	Zhou	Li
俱	絺	羅、	離	婆	多、	周	利
Pan	Tuo	Qie	Nan	Tuo	O	Nan	Tuo
槃	陀	伽、	難	陀、	阿	難	陀、
Luo	Hou	Luo	Jiao	Fan	Bo	Ti	Bin
羅	睺	羅、	憍	梵	波	提、	賓
Tou	Lu	Po	Luo	Duo	Jia	Liu	Tuo
頭	盧	頗	羅	墮、	迦	留	陀
Yi	Mo	He	Jie	Bin	Nuo	Bo	Ju
夷、	摩	訶	劫	賓	那、	薄	拘
Luo	O	Nou	Lou	Tuo	Ru	Shi	Deng
羅、	阿	耨	樓	馱，	如	是	等
Zhu	Da	Di	Zi	Bing	Zhu	Pu	Sa
諸	大	弟	子，	並	諸	菩	薩
Mo	He	Sa	Wen	Shu	Shi	Li	Fa
摩	訶	薩，	文	殊	師	利	法

[...] such as the elders Sariputra, Mahamaudgalyayana, Mahakasyapa, Mahakatyayana, Mahakausthila, Revata, Suddhipanthaka, Nanda, Ananda, Rahula, Gavampati, Pindola Bharadvaja, Kalodayin, Mahakapphina, Vakkula, Aniruddha and other great disciples like these. [...]

Wang Zi O Yi Duo Pu Sa Qian
王子、阿逸多菩薩、乾

Tuo He Ti Pu Sa Chang Jīng Jìn
陀訶提菩薩、常精進

Pu Sa Yu Ru Shi Deng Zhu Da
菩薩，與如是等諸大

Pu Sa Ji Shi Ti Huan Yin Deng
菩薩，及釋提桓因等

Wu Liang Zhu Tian Da Zhong Ju
無量諸天大眾俱。

Er Shi Fo Gao Zhang Lao She Li
爾時，佛告長老舍利

Fo
弗：

Cong Shi Xi Fang Guo Shi Wan Yi
「從是西方，過十萬億

Fo Tu You Shi Jie Ming Yue Ji
佛土，有世界名曰極

Le Qi Tu You Fo Hao O Mi
樂。其土有佛，號阿彌

Tuo Jin Xian Zai Shuo Fa She Li
陀，今現在說法。舍利

[...] Also, the bodhisattvas, mahasattvas, Dharma Prince Manjusri, Ajita Bodhisattva, Gandhahastin Bodhisattva, Nityodyukta Bodhisattva and other great bodhisattvas like these—as well as Sakra Devanam Indra and immeasurable other heavenly beings—were all in the great assembly.

At the time, the Buddha told the elder Sariputra, "West of here, passing beyond hundreds of thousands of millions of Buddhas' lands, there is a world called 'Ultimate Bliss.' In that land there is a Buddha named Amitabha who has now manifested there to teach the Dharma.

Fo	Bi	Tu	He	Gu	Ming	Wei	Ji
弗！	彼	土	何	故	名	為	極
Le	Qi	Guo	Zhong	Sheng	Wu	You	Zhong
樂？	其	國	眾	生	無	有	眾
Ku	Dan	Shou	Zhu	Le	Gu	Ming	Ji
苦，	但	受	諸	樂，	故	名	極
Le	You	She	Li	Fo	Ji	Le	Guo
樂。	又	舍	利	弗！	極	樂	國
Tu	Qi	Chong	Lan	Xun	Qi	Chong	Luo
土，	七	重	欄	楯、	七	重	羅
Wang	Qi	Chong	Hang	Shu	Jie	Shi	Si
網、	七	重	行	樹，	皆	是	四
Bao	Zhou	Za	Wei	Rao	Shi	Gu	Bi
寶	周	帀	圍	繞，	是	故	彼
Guo	Ming	Wei	Ji	Le			
國	名	為	極	樂。			
You	She	Li	Fo	Ji	Le	Guo	Tu
「又	舍	利	弗！	極	樂	國	土
You	Qi	Bao	Chi	Ba	Gong	De	Shui
有	七	寶	池，	八	功	德	水，
Chong	Man	Qi	Zhong	Chi	Di	Chun	Yi
充	滿	其	中，	池	底	純	以

"Sariputra, why is that land called 'Ultimate Bliss'? The sentient beings in that land are without any kind of suffering, and only enjoy various kinds of happiness, therefore it is called Ultimate Bliss.

"Furthermore, Sariputra, completely circling the Land of Ultimate Bliss are seven tiers of railings, seven layers of netting, and seven rows of trees, which are all made of the four treasures. For this reason, that land is called Ultimate Bliss.

"Furthermore, Sariputra, in the Land of Ultimate Bliss there are ponds of seven treasures that are filled with the water of eight virtues, and the ground on the bottom of the ponds is [...]

Jin	Sha	Bu	Di	Si	Bian	Jie	Dao
金	沙	布	地；	四	邊	階	道，
Jin	Yin	Liu	Li	Bo	Li	He	Cheng
金、	銀、	瑠	璃、	玻	瓈	合	成。
Shang	You	Lou	Ge	Yi	Yi	Jin	Yin
上	有	樓	閣，	亦	以	金、	銀、
Liu	Li	Bo	Li	Che	Qu	Chi	Zhu
瑠	璃、	玻	瓈、	硨	磲、	赤	珠、
Ma	Nao	Er	Yan	Shi	Zhi	Chi	Zhong
瑪	瑙，	而	嚴	飾	之。	池	中
Lian	Hua	Da	Ru	Che	Lun	Qing	Se
蓮	華，	大	如	車	輪，	青	色
Qing	Guang	Huang	Se	Huang	Guang	Chi	Se
青	光，	黃	色	黃	光，	赤	色
Chi	Guang	Bai	Se	Bai	Guang	Wei	Miao
赤	光，	白	色	白	光，	微	妙
Xiang	Jie	She	Li	Fo	Ji	Le	Guo
香	潔。	舍	利	弗！	極	樂	國
Tu	Cheng	Jiu	Ru	Shi	Gong	De	Zhuang
土	成	就	如	是	功	德	莊
Yan							
嚴。							

[...] covered solely by gold sand. On the four sides, there are stairways composed of gold, silver, lapis lazuli, and crystal. Above, there are towered pavilions that have gold, silver, lapis lazuli, crystal, nacre, red pearls, and carnelian magnificently adorning them.

"In the ponds there are lotus flowers as large as carriage wheels that are blue colored with a blue sheen, yellow colored with a yellow sheen, red colored with a red sheen, and white colored with a white sheen. They are fine, wondrous, fragrant, and pure. Sariputra, the Land of Ultimate Bliss is complete with virtues and adornments like these.

You	She	Li	Fo	Bi	Fo	Guo	Tu
「又	舍	利	弗！	彼	佛	國	土，
Chang	Zuo	Tian	Yue	Huang	Jin	Wei	Di
常	作	天	樂，	黃	金	為	地，
Zhou	Ye	Liu	Shi	Yu	Tian	Man	Tuo
晝	夜	六	時，	雨	天	曼	陀
Luo	Hua	Qi	Tu	Zhong	Sheng	Chang	Yi
羅	華。	其	土	眾	生，	常	以
Qing	Dan	Ge	Yi	Yi	Ge	Cheng	Zhong
清	旦，	各	以	衣	裓，	盛	眾
Miao	Hua	Gong	Yang	Ta	Fang	Shi	Wan
妙	華，	供	養	他	方	十	萬
Yi	Fo	Ji	Yi	Shi	Shi	Huan	Dao
億	佛，	即	以	食	時，	還	到
Ben	Guo	Fan	Shi	Jing	Xing	She	Li
本	國，	飯	食	經	行。	舍	利
Fo	Ji	Le	Guo	Tu	Cheng	Jiu	Ru
弗！	極	樂	國	土	成	就	如
Shi	Gong	De	Zhuang	Yan			
是	功	德	莊	嚴。			
Fu	Ci	She	Li	Fo	Bi	Guo	Chang
「復	次	舍	利	弗！	彼	國	常

"Furthermore, Sariputra, in that Buddha land heavenly music constantly plays, and the ground is made of gold. Throughout the six periods of day and night, heavenly mandarava flowers rain down. Early in the morning, the sentient beings in that land always fill the hem of their robes with many wondrous flowers and make offerings to the hundreds of thousands of millions of Buddhas in the other directions, and return by mealtime to eat their food and walk in meditation. Sariputra, the Land of Ultimate Bliss is complete with virtues and adornments like these.

You	Zhong	Zhong	Qi	Miao	Za	Se	Zhi
有	種	種	奇	妙	雜	色	之
Niao	Bai	He	Kong	Que	Ying	Wu	She
鳥，	白	鶴、	孔	雀、	鸚	鵡、	舍
Li	Jia	Ling	Pin	Qie	Gong	Ming	Zhi
利、	迦	陵	頻	伽、	共	命	之
Niao	Shi	Zhu	Zhong	Niao	Zhou	Ye	Liu
鳥。	是	諸	眾	鳥，	晝	夜	六
Shi	Chu	He	Ya	Yin	Qi	Yin	Yan
時，	出	和	雅	音。	其	音	演
Chang	Wu	Gen	Wu	Li	Qi	Pu	Ti
暢，	五	根、	五	力、	七	菩	提
Fen	Ba	Sheng	Dao	Fen	Ru	Shi	Deng
分、	八	聖	道	分，	如	是	等
Fa	Qi	Tu	Zhong	Sheng	Wen	Shi	Yin
法。	其	土	眾	生，	聞	是	音
Yi	Jie	Xi	Nian	Fo	Nian	Fa	Nian
已，	皆	悉	念	佛、	念	法、	念
Seng	She	Li	Fo	Ru	Wu	Wei	Ci
僧。	舍	利	弗！	汝	勿	謂	此
Niao	Shi	Shi	Zui	Bao	Suo	Sheng	Suo
鳥	實	是	罪	報	所	生。	所

"Moreover, Sariputra, in that land there are always various kinds of rare multicolored birds, such as snow cranes, peacocks, parrots, saris, kalavinkas, and birds that are conjoined. Throughout the six periods of day and night, all of these birds sing in harmony and with elegant sound. These sounds proclaim the five faculties, the five strengths, the seven factors of awakening, the Noble Eightfold Path, and other teachings like these. After hearing these sounds, all the sentient beings in that land are fully mindful of the Buddha, the Dharma, and the Sangha.

"Sariputra, you should not say that these birds are actually born because of the karmic effects of past offenses. [...]

Yi	Zhe	He	Bi	Fo	Guo	Tu	Wu
以	者	何？	彼	佛	國	土，	無
San	E	Dao	She	Li	Fo	Qi	Fo
三	惡	道。	舍	利	弗！	其	佛
Guo	Tu	Shang	Wu	E	Dao	Zhi	Ming
國	土，	尚	無	惡	道	之	名，
He	Kuang	You	Shi	Shi	Zhu	Zhong	Niao
何	況	有	實？	是	諸	眾	鳥，
Jie	Shi	O	Mi	Tuo	Fo	Yu	Ling
皆	是	阿	彌	陀	佛，	欲	令
Fa	Yin	Xuan	Liu	Bian	Hua	Suo	Zuo
法	音	宣	流，	變	化	所	作。
She	Li	Fo	Bi	Fo	Guo	Tu	Wei
舍	利	弗！	彼	佛	國	土，	微
Feng	Chui	Dong	Zhu	Bao	Hang	Shu	Ji
風	吹	動，	諸	寶	行	樹，	及
Bao	Luo	Wang	Chu	Wei	Miao	Yin	Pi
寶	羅	網，	出	微	妙	音，	譬
Ru	Bai	Qian	Zhong	Yue	Tong	Shi	Ju
如	百	千	種	樂，	同	時	俱
Zuo	Wen	Shi	Yin	Zhe	Zi	Ran	Jie
作。	聞	是	音	者，	自	然	皆

[...] Why is this? Because that Buddha land is without the three lower realms. Sariputra, that Buddha land does not even have the names of the three lower realms, so how could they exist? All of these birds are transformationally produced through Amitabha Buddha's intention to cause the sounds of the Dharma to be widely circulated. Sariputra, when gentle breezes blow in that Buddha land, all of the rows of jeweled trees and jeweled nets let out a subtle, wondrous sound similar to hundreds of thousands of types of music playing simultaneously. [...]

Sheng	Nian	Fo	Nian	Fa	Nian	Seng	Zhi
生	念	佛、	念	法、	念	僧	之
Xin	She	Li	Fo	Qi	Fo	Guo	Tu
心。	舍	利	弗！	其	佛	國	土
Cheng	Jiu	Ru	Shi	Gong	De	Zhuang	Yan
成	就	如	是	功	德	莊	嚴。
She	Li	Fo	Yu	Ru	Yi	Yun	He
「舍	利	弗！	於	汝	意	云	何？
Bi	Fo	He	Gu	Hao	O	Mi	Tuo
彼	佛	何	故	號	阿	彌	陀？
She	Li	Fo	Bi	Fo	Guang	Ming	Wu
舍	利	弗！	彼	佛	光	明	無
Liang	Zhao	Shi	Fang	Guo	Wu	Suo	Zhang
量，	照	十	方	國，	無	所	障
Ai	Shi	Gu	Hao	Wei	O	Mi	Tuo
礙，	是	故	號	為	阿	彌	陀。
You	She	Li	Fo	Bi	Fo	Shou	Ming
又	舍	利	弗！	彼	佛	壽	命
Ji	Qi	Ren	Min	Wu	Liang	Wu	Bian
及	其	人	民，	無	量	無	邊
A	Seng	Qi	Jie	Gu	Ming	O	Mi
阿	僧	祇	劫，	故	名	阿	彌

[...] Those who hear the sounds will spontaneously give rise to a mind that is mindful of the Buddha, the Dharma, and the Sangha. Sariputra, that Buddha land is complete with virtues and adornments like these.

"Sariputra, what do you think? Why is that Buddha named Amitabha?

"Sariputra, that Buddha's brilliant radiance is immeasurable and illuminates the lands of the ten directions without any obstruction, therefore he is named Amitabha.

"Furthermore, Sariputra, the lifespan of that Buddha and his people lasts for immeasurable, infinite *asamkhya*[2] *kalpas.*[3] Therefore, he is called Amitabha.

2. A Sanskrit term that literally means incalculable. A very large number unit. It is the sixtieth number of successively larger numbers with each one ten times greater than the preceding one.
3. An Indic unit of time, a very long period of time.

Tuo	She	Li	Fo	O	Mi	Tuo	Fo
陀。	舍	利	弗！	阿	彌	陀	佛
Cheng	Fo	Yi	Lai	Yu	Jin	Shi	Jie
成	佛	已	來，	於	今	十	劫。
You	She	Li	Fo	Bi	Fo	You	Wu
又	舍	利	弗！	彼	佛	有	無
Liang	Wu	Bian	Sheng	Wen	Di	Zi	Jie
量	無	邊	聲	聞	弟	子，	皆
O	Luo	Han	Fei	Shi	Suan	Shu	Zhi
阿	羅	漢，	非	是	算	數	之
Suo	Neng	Zhi	Zhu	Pu	Sa	Zhong	Yi
所	能	知。	諸	菩	薩	眾，	亦
Fu	Ru	Shi	She	Li	Fo	Bi	Fo
復	如	是。	舍	利	弗！	彼	佛
Guo	Tu	Cheng	Jiu	Ru	Shi	Gong	De
國	土，	成	就	如	是	功	德
Zhuang	Yan						
莊	嚴。						
You	She	Li	Fo	Ji	Le	Guo	Tu
「又	舍	利	弗！	極	樂	國	土
Zhong	Sheng	Sheng	Zhe	Jie	Shi	O	Pi
眾	生	生	者，	皆	是	阿	鞞

"Sariputra, it has been ten *kalpas* since Amitabha Buddha attained Buddhahood.

"Furthermore, Sariputra, that Buddha has immeasurable, infinite *sravaka*[4] disciples, who are all arhats and whose numbers cannot be known by calculation. All of the bodhisattvas are also like this. Sariputra, that Buddha land is complete with virtues and adornments like these.

4. One who has heard. One who has been liberated from the cycle of birth and death after listening to the Buddha's teachings but does not seek to become a Buddha.

Ba	Zhi	Qi	Zhong	Duo	You	Yi	Sheng
跋	致。	其	中	多	有	一	生
Bu	Chu	Qi	Shu	Shen	Duo	Fei	Shi
補	處，	其	數	甚	多，	非	是
Suan	Shu	Suo	Neng	Zhi	Zhi	Dan	Ke
算	數	所	能	知	之，	但	可
Yi	Wu	Liang	Wu	Bian	A	Seng	Qi
以	無	量	無	邊	阿	僧	祇
Shuo	She	Li	Fo	Zhong	Sheng	Wen	Zhe
說。	舍	利	弗！	眾	生	聞	者，
Ying	Dang	Fa	Yuan	Yuan	Sheng	Bi	Guo
應	當	發	願，	願	生	彼	國。
Suo	Yi	Zhe	He	De	Yu	Ru	Shi
所	以	者	何？	得	與	如	是
Zhu	Shang	Shan	Ren	Ju	Hui	Yi	Chu
諸	上	善	人	俱	會	一	處。
She	Li	Fo	Bu	Ke	Yi	Shao	Shan
「舍	利	弗！	不	可	以	少	善
Gen	Fu	De	Yin	Yuan	De	Sheng	Bi
根	福	德	因	緣，	得	生	彼
Guo	She	Li	Fo	Ruo	You	Shan	Nan
國。	舍	利	弗！	若	有	善	男

"Furthermore, Sariputra, the sentient beings who are born in the Land of Ultimate Bliss are all *avaivartikas*,[5] and among them there are many who will become Buddhas in one more rebirth. Their numbers are extremely vast, and cannot be known by calculation. One could only speak of them in terms of immeasurable, infinite *asamkhyas*.

"Sariputra, sentient beings who hear this should set forth a vow to be reborn in that land. Why is this? Because they will be able to meet with all of the utmost virtuous people like these in a single place.

"Sariputra, it is not possible to obtain rebirth in that land with few wholesome roots and meritorious causes and conditions. [...]

5. A bodhisattva who will not regress on the path to Buddhahood.

Zi	Shan	Nü	Ren	Wen	Shuo	O	Mi
子、	善	女	人，	聞	說	阿	彌
Tuo	Fo	Zhi	Chi	Ming	Hao	Ruo	Yi
陀	佛，	執	持	名	號，	若	一
Ri	Ruo	Er	Ri	Ruo	San	Ri	Ruo
日、	若	二	日、	若	三	日、	若
Si	Ri	Ruo	Wu	Ri	Ruo	Liu	Ri
四	日、	若	五	日、	若	六	日、
Ruo	Qi	Ri	Yi	Xin	Bu	Luan	Qi
若	七	日，	一	心	不	亂，	其
Ren	Lin	Ming	Zhong	Shi	O	Mi	Tuo
人	臨	命	終	時，	阿	彌	陀
Fo	Yu	Zhu	Sheng	Zhong	Xian	Zai	Qi
佛，	與	諸	聖	眾，	現	在	其
Qian	Shi	Ren	Zhong	Shi	Xin	Bu	Dian
前。	是	人	終	時，	心	不	顛
Dao	Ji	De	Wang	Sheng	O	Mi	Tuo
倒，	即	得	往	生	阿	彌	陀
Fo	Ji	Le	Guo	Tu	She	Li	Fo
佛，	極	樂	國	土。	舍	利	弗！
Wo	Jian	Shi	Li	Gu	Shuo	Ci	Yan
我	見	是	利，	故	說	此	言；

[...] Sariputra, if good men and women hear Amitabha Buddha mentioned and hold firmly to his name for one day, two days, three, four, five, six, or seven days, wholeheartedly without distraction, then when these people are near the end of life, Amitabha Buddha will appear in front of them with a host of sages.

"In their final moments, if the minds of these people are not distorted, then they will be reborn in Amitabha's Land of Ultimate Bliss.

Ruo	You	Zhong	Sheng	Wen	Shi	Shuo	Zhe
若	有	眾	生，	聞	是	說	者，
Ying	Dang	Fa	Yuan	Sheng	Bi	Guo	Tu
應	當	發	願，	生	彼	國	土。
She	Li	Fo	Ru	Wo	Jin	Zhe	Zan
「舍	利	弗！	如	我	今	者，	讚
Tan	O	Mi	Tuo	Fo	Bu	Ke	Si
歎	阿	彌	陀	佛，	不	可	思
Yi	Gong	De	Zhi	Li	Dong	Fang	Yi
議	功	德	之	利。	東	方	亦
You	O	Chu	Pi	Fo	Xu	Mi	Xiang
有	阿	閦	鞞	佛、	須	彌	相
Fo	Da	Xu	Mi	Fo	Xu	Mi	Guang
佛、	大	須	彌	佛、	須	彌	光
Fo	Miao	Yin	Fo	Ru	Shi	Deng	Heng
佛、	妙	音	佛，	如	是	等	恒
He	Sha	Shu	Zhu	Fo	Ge	Yu	Qi
河	沙	數	諸	佛。	各	於	其
Guo	Chu	Guang	Chang	She	Xiang	Pian	Fu
國，	出	廣	長	舌	相，	遍	覆
San	Qian	Da	Qian	Shi	Jie	Shuo	Cheng
三	千	大	千	世	界，	說	誠

"Sariputra, I recognize these benefits, therefore I proclaim these words: 'If there are sentient beings who hear this spoken, they should set forth a vow to be born in that land.'

"Sariputra, similar to me now, there are also those in the eastern region who praise the inconceivable virtues of Amitabha Buddha, such as Aksobya Buddha, Sumeru Emblem Buddha, Great Sumeru Buddha, Sumeru Light Buddha, Wondrous Voice Buddha, and other Buddhas like these who are as numerous as grains of sand in the Ganges River. [...]

Shi	Yan	Ru	Deng	Zhong	Sheng	Dang	Xin
實	言：『	汝	等	眾	生，	當	信
Shi	Cheng	Zan	Bu	Ke	Si	Yi	Gong
是	「稱	讚	不	可	思	議	功
De	Yi	Qie	Zhu	Fo	Suo	Hu	Nian
德	一	切	諸	佛	所	護	念
Jing							
經。」』							
She	Li	Fo	Nan	Fang	Shi	Jie	You
「舍	利	弗！	南	方	世	界	有
Ri	Yue	Deng	Fo	Ming	Wen	Guang	Fo
日	月	燈	佛、	名	聞	光	佛、
Da	Yan	Jian	Fo	Xu	Mi	Deng	Fo
大	燄	肩	佛、	須	彌	燈	佛、
Wu	Liang	Jing	Jin	Fo	Ru	Shi	Deng
無	量	精	進	佛，	如	是	等
Heng	He	Sha	Shu	Zhu	Fo	Ge	Yu
恒	河	沙	數	諸	佛。	各	於
Qi	Guo	Chu	Guang	Chang	She	Xiang	Pian
其	國，	出	廣	長	舌	相，	遍
Fu	San	Qian	Da	Qian	Shi	Jie	Shuo
覆	三	千	大	千	世	界，	說

[...] From their own lands, they each extend their characteristic long, broad tongues covering everywhere in the three thousandfold world systems[6] and speak these sincere and true words: 'Sentient beings, you should believe in the *Praising the Inconceivable Virtues Which All Buddhas Have Protected Sutra*.'

"Sariputra, in the southern region there is Sun Moon Beacon Buddha, Renowned Light Buddha, Great Blazing Shoulders Buddha, Sumeru Beacon Buddha, Immeasurable Diligence Buddha, and other Buddhas like these who are as numerous [...]

6. According to Buddhist cosmology, a world consists of a Mount Sumeru at its center surrounded by nine mountains, eight oceans, four continents, sun, moon, and star. A group of one thousand such worlds is called a "small world system," one thousand small world systems equal a "medium world system," and one thousand medium world systems equal a "large world system." A three thousandfold world system is a combination of these three types of world systems.

Cheng	Shi	Yan	Ru	Deng	Zhong	Sheng	Dang
誠	實	言：『	汝	等	眾	生，	當
Xin	Shi	Cheng	Zan	Bu	Ke	Si	Yi
信	是	「稱	讚	不	可	思	議
Gong	De	Yi	Qie	Zhu	Fo	Suo	Hu
功	德	一	切	諸	佛	所	護
Nian	Jing						
念	經。」』						
She	Li	Fo	Xi	Fang	Shi	Jie	You
「舍	利	弗！	西	方	世	界	有
Wu	Liang	Shou	Fo	Wu	Liang	Xiang	Fo
無	量	壽	佛、	無	量	相	佛、
Wu	Liang	Chuang	Fo	Da	Guang	Fo	Da
無	量	幢	佛、	大	光	佛、	大
Ming	Fo	Bao	Xiang	Fo	Jing	Guang	Fo
明	佛、	寶	相	佛、	淨	光	佛，
Ru	Shi	Deng	Heng	He	Sha	Shu	Zhu
如	是	等	恒	河	沙	數	諸
Fo	Ge	Yu	Qi	Guo	Chu	Guang	Chang
佛。	各	於	其	國，	出	廣	長
She	Xiang	Pian	Fu	San	Qian	Da	Qian
舌	相，	遍	覆	三	千	大	千

[...] as grains of sand in the Ganges River. From their own lands, they each extend their characteristic long, broad tongues covering everywhere in the three thousandfold world systems and speak these sincere and true words: 'Sentient beings, you should believe in the *Praising the Inconceivable Virtues Which All Buddhas Have Protected Sutra*.'

"Sariputra, in the western region there is Immeasurable Life Buddha, Immeasurable Emblem Buddha, Immeasurable Banner Buddha, Great Light Buddha, Great Brilliance Buddha, Treasure Emblem Buddha, Pure Light Buddha, and other Buddhas like these who are as numerous as grains of sand in the Ganges River. From their own lands, they each extend their characteristic long, broad tongues covering everywhere [...]

Shi Jie Shuo Cheng Shi Yan Ru Deng

世界，說誠實言：『汝等

Zhong Sheng Dang Xin Shi Cheng Zan Bu

眾生，當信是「稱讚不

Ke Si Yi Gong De Yi Qie Zhu

可思議功德一切諸

Fo Suo Hu Nian Jing

佛所護念經。」』

She Li Fo Bei Fang Shi Jie You

「舍利弗！北方世界有

Yan Jian Fo Zui Sheng Yin Fo Nan

燄肩佛、最勝音佛、難

Ju Fo Ri Sheng Fo Wang Ming Fo

沮佛、日生佛、網明佛，

Ru Shi Deng Heng He Sha Shu Zhu

如是等恒河沙數諸

Fo Ge Yu Qi Guo Chu Guang Chang

佛。各於其國，出廣長

She Xiang Pian Fu San Qian Da Qian

舌相，遍覆三千大千

Shi Jie Shuo Cheng Shi Yan Ru Deng

世界，說誠實言：『汝等

[...] in the three thousandfold world systems and speak these sincere and true words: 'Sentient beings, you should believe in the *Praising the Inconceivable Virtues Which All Buddhas Have Protected Sutra.'*

"Sariputra, in the northern region there is Blazing Shoulders Buddha, Most Excellent Voice Buddha, Unstoppable Buddha, Sun Birth Buddha, Net Brilliance Buddha, and other Buddhas like these who are as numerous as grains of sand in the Ganges River. From their own lands, they each extend their characteristic long, broad tongues covering everywhere in the three thousandfold world systems and speak these sincere and true words: [...]

Zhong Sheng Dang Xin Shi Cheng Zan Bu
眾 生， 當 信 是 「稱 讚 不

Ke Si Yi Gong De Yi Qie Zhu
可 思 議 功 德 一 切 諸

Fo Suo Hu Nian Jing
佛 所 護 念 經。」』

She Li Fo Xia Fang Shi Jie You
「舍 利 弗！ 下 方 世 界 有

Shi Zi Fo Ming Wen Fo Ming Guang
師 子 佛、 名 聞 佛、 名 光

Fo Da Mo Fo Fa Chuang Fo Chi
佛、 達 摩 佛、 法 幢 佛、 持

Fa Fo Ru Shi Deng Heng He Sha
法 佛， 如 是 等 恒 河 沙

Shu Zhu Fo Ge Yu Qi Guo Chu
數 諸 佛。 各 於 其 國， 出

Guang Chang She Xiang Pian Fu San Qian
廣 長 舌 相， 遍 覆 三 千

Da Qian Shi Jie Shuo Cheng Shi Yan
大 千 世 界， 說 誠 實 言：

Ru Deng Zhong Sheng Dang Xin Shi Cheng
『汝 等 眾 生， 當 信 是 「稱

[...] 'Sentient beings, you should believe in the *Praising the Inconceivable Virtues Which All Buddhas Have Protected Sutra.*'

"Sariputra, in the lower region there is Lion Buddha, Renowned Buddha, Acclaimed Light Buddha, Dharma Buddha, Dharma Banner Buddha, Upholding the Dharma Buddha, and other Buddhas like these who are as numerous as grains of sand in the Ganges River. From their own lands, they each extend their characteristic long, broad tongues covering everywhere in the three thousandfold world systems and speak these sincere and true words: 'Sentient beings, you should believe in [...]

Zan	Bu	Ke	Si	Yi	Gong	De	Yi
讚	不	可	思	議	功	德	一
Qie	Zhu	Fo	Suo	Hu	Nian	Jing	
切	諸	佛	所	護	念	經。」』	
She	Li	Fo	Shang	Fang	Shi	Jie	You
「舍	利	弗！	上	方	世	界	有
Fan	Yin	Fo	Su	Wang	Fo	Xiang	Shang
梵	音	佛、	宿	王	佛、	香	上
Fo	Xiang	Guang	Fo	Da	Yan	Jian	Fo
佛、	香	光	佛、	大	燄	肩	佛、
Za	Se	Bao	Hua	Yan	Shen	Fo	Suo
雜	色	寶	華	嚴	身	佛、	娑
Luo	Shu	Wang	Fo	Bao	Hua	De	Fo
羅	樹	王	佛、	寶	華	德	佛、
Jian	Yi	Qie	Yi	Fo	Ru	Xu	Mi
見	一	切	義	佛、	如	須	彌
Shan	Fo	Ru	Shi	Deng	Heng	He	Sha
山	佛，	如	是	等	恒	河	沙
Shu	Zhu	Fo	Ge	Yu	Qi	Guo	Chu
數	諸	佛。	各	於	其	國，	出
Guang	Chang	She	Xiang	Pian	Fu	San	Qian
廣	長	舌	相，	遍	覆	三	千

[...] the *Praising the Inconceivable Virtues Which All Buddhas Have Protected Sutra.*'

"Sariputra, in the upper region there is Brahma Voice Buddha, Constellation King Buddha, Foremost Fragrance Buddha, Fragrance and Light Buddha, Great Blazing Shoulders Buddha, Multicolored Jeweled Flower Adornment Body Buddha, King of the Sala Tree Buddha, Jeweled Flower Virtue Buddha, Discerning All Meanings Buddha, Sumeru-Like Buddha, and other Buddhas like these who are as numerous as grains of sand in the Ganges River. From their own lands, they each extend their characteristic long, broad tongues covering everywhere in the three thousandfold world systems [...]

Da	Qian	Shi	Jie	Shuo	Cheng	Shi	Yan
大	千	世	界，	說	誠	實	言：
Ru	Deng	Zhong	Sheng	Dang	Xin	Shi	Cheng
『汝	等	眾	生，	當	信	是	「稱
Zan	Bu	Ke	Si	Yi	Gong	De	Yi
讚	不	可	思	議	功	德	一
Qie	Zhu	Fo	Suo	Hu	Nian	Jing	
切	諸	佛	所	護	念	經。」』	
She	Li	Fo	Yu	Ru	Yi	Yun	He
「舍	利	弗！	於	汝	意	云	何？
He	Gu	Ming	Wei	Yi	Qie	Zhu	Fo
何	故	名	為	『一	切	諸	佛
Suo	Hu	Nian	Jing	She	Li	Fo	Ruo
所	護	念	經』？	舍	利	弗！	若
You	Shan	Nan	Zi	Shan	Nü	Ren	Wen
有	善	男	子、	善	女	人，	聞
Shi	Jing	Shou	Chi	Zhe	Ji	Wen	Zhu
是	經	受	持	者，	及	聞	諸
Fo	Ming	Zhe	Shi	Zhu	Shan	Nan	Zi
佛	名	者，	是	諸	善	男	子、
Shan	Nü	Ren	Jie	Wei	Yi	Qie	Zhu
善	女	人，	皆	為	一	切	諸

[...] and speak these sincere and true words: 'Sentient beings, you should believe in the *Praising the Inconceivable Virtues Which All Buddhas Have Protected Sutra*.'

"Sariputra, what do you think? Why is it called the *Praising the Inconceivable Virtues Which All Buddhas Have Protected Sutra*?

"Sariputra, if there are those good men and women who hear this sutra and receive and retain it, and hear the name of all the Buddhas, then all of these good men and women are protected and kept in mind by all Buddhas. [...]

Fo	Zhi	Suo	Hu	Nian	Jie	De	Bu
佛	之	所	護	念，	皆	得	不
Tui	Zhuan	Yu	O	Nou	Duo	Luo	San
退	轉	於	阿	耨	多	羅	三
Miao	San	Pu	Ti	Shi	Gu	She	Li
藐	三	菩	提。	是	故	舍	利
Fo	Ru	Deng	Jie	Dang	Xin	Shou	Wo
弗！	汝	等	皆	當	信	受	我
Yu	Ji	Zhu	Fo	Suo	Shuo		
語，	及	諸	佛	所	說。		
She	Li	Fo	Ruo	You	Ren	Yi	Fa
「舍	利	弗！	若	有	人，	已	發
Yuan	Jin	Fa	Yuan	Dang	Fa	Yuan	Yu
願、	今	發	願、	當	發	願，	欲
Sheng	O	Mi	Tuo	Fo	Guo	Zhe	Shi
生	阿	彌	陀	佛	國	者，	是
Zhu	Ren	Deng	Jie	De	Bu	Tui	Zhuan
諸	人	等，	皆	得	不	退	轉
Yu	O	Nou	Duo	Luo	San	Miao	San
於	阿	耨	多	羅	三	藐	三
Pu	Ti	Yu	Bi	Guo	Tu	Ruo	Yi
菩	提，	於	彼	國	土	若	已

[...] All of them will attain non-regression from *anuttara-samyak-sambodhi.*[7] For this reason, Sariputra, all of you should believe and receive my words, and those of all Buddhas.

"Sariputra, if there are those who have already put forth a vow, or who are presently setting forth a vow, or who will set forth a vow wanting to be reborn in the Land of Amitabha Buddha, then all of these people will attain non-regression from *anuttara-samyak-sambodhi,* [...]

7. A Sanskrit term meaning complete, unexcelled enlightenment; an attribute of all Buddhas.

Sheng	Ruo	Jin	Sheng	Ruo	Dang	Sheng	Shi
生、	若	今	生、	若	當	生，	是
Gu	She	Li	Fo	Zhu	Shan	Nan	Zi
故	舍	利	弗！	諸	善	男	子、
Shan	Nü	Ren	Ruo	You	Xin	Zhe	Ying
善	女	人，	若	有	信	者，	應
Dang	Fa	Yuan	Sheng	Bi	Guo	Tu	
當	發	願，	生	彼	國	土。	
She	Li	Fo	Ru	Wo	Jin	Zhe	Cheng
「舍	利	弗！	如	我	今	者，	稱
Zan	Zhu	Fo	Bu	Ke	Si	Yi	Gong
讚	諸	佛	不	可	思	議	功
De	Bi	Zhu	Fo	Deng	Yi	Cheng	Zan
德，	彼	諸	佛	等，	亦	稱	讚
Wo	Bu	Ke	Si	Yi	Gong	De	Er
我	不	可	思	議	功	德，	而
Zuo	Shi	Yan	Shi	Jia	Mou	Ni	Fo
作	是	言：	『釋	迦	牟	尼	佛
Neng	Wei	Shen	Nan	Xi	You	Zhi	Shi
能	為	甚	難	希	有	之	事，
Neng	Yu	Suo	Po	Guo	Tu	Wu	Zhuo
能	於	娑	婆	國	土，	五	濁

[...] whether they are already born, presently being born, or will be born in that land. For this reason, Sariputra, if there are those good men and women who believe, they should set forth a vow to be reborn in that land.

"Sariputra, just as I now praise the inconceivable virtues of all Buddhas, those Buddhas also commend my inconceivable virtues, proclaiming these words: 'Sakyamuni Buddha is able to accomplish extremely difficult and rare feats. In the Saha land amid [...]

E	Shi	Jie	Zhuo	Jian	Zhuo	Fan	Nao
惡	世，	劫	濁、	見	濁、	煩	惱
Zhuo	Zhong	Sheng	Zhuo	Ming	Zhuo	Zhong	De
濁、	眾	生	濁、	命	濁	中，	得
O	Nou	Duo	Luo	San	Miao	San	Pu
阿	耨	多	羅	三	藐	三	菩
Ti	Wei	Zhu	Zhong	Sheng	Shuo	Shi	Yi
提，	為	諸	眾	生，	說	是	一
Qie	Shi	Jian	Nan	Xin	Zhi	Fa	She
切	世	間	難	信	之	法。』	舍
Li	Fo	Dang	Zhi	Wo	Yu	Wu	Zhuo
利	弗！	當	知	我	於	五	濁
E	Shi	Xing	Ci	Nan	Shi	De	O
惡	世，	行	此	難	事，	得	阿
Nou	Duo	Luo	San	Miao	San	Pu	Ti
耨	多	羅	三	藐	三	菩	提，
Wei	Yi	Qie	Shi	Jian	Shuo	Ci	Nan
為	一	切	世	間	說	此	難
Xin	Zhi	Fa	Shi	Wei	Shen	Nan	
信	之	法，	是	為	甚	難。」	
Fo	Shuo	Ci	Jing	Yi	She	Li	Fo
佛	說	此	經	已，	舍	利	弗

[...] the evil period of five degenerations—*kalpa* degeneration, view degeneration, affliction degeneration, sentient being degeneration, and lifespan degeneration—he is able to attain *anuttara-samyak-sambodhi*. For the sake of all sentient beings, he teaches this Dharma that this world finds hard to believe.'

"Sariputra, you should know, I have practiced these difficult feats during the evil period of five degenerations, attaining *anuttara-samyak-sambodhi*, and have taught this Dharma that the world finds hard to believe. This is extremely difficult."

Ji	Zhu	Bi	Qiu	Yi	Qie	Shi	Jian
及	諸	比	丘，	一	切	世	間
Tian	Ren	O	Xiu	Luo	Deng	Wen	Fo
天、	人、	阿	修	羅	等，	聞	佛
Suo	Shuo	Huan	Xi	Xin	Shou	Zuo	Li
所	說，	歡	喜	信	受，	作	禮
Er	Qu						
而	去。						

Fo Shuo O Mi Tuo Jing

佛 說 阿 彌 陀 經

After the Buddha spoke this sutra, Sariputra and all of the *bhiksus*, and heavenly beings, humans, and *asuras*[8] of all the worldly realms heard what the Buddha said, rejoiced in it, and faithfully accepted it. They made obeisance and then departed.

[Thus ends] the *Amitabha Sutra*
as Discoursed by the Buddha

8. Also known as non-heaven; they are prone to hatred, arrogance, and suspicion.

Wang Sheng Zhou
往 生 咒

Ba	Yi	Qie	Ye	Zhang	Gen	Ben	De
拔	一	切	業	障	根	本	得
Sheng	Jing	Tu	Tuo	Luo	Ni		
生	淨	土	陀	羅	尼		

Na	Mo	O	Mi	Duo	Po	Ye	○
南	無	阿	彌	多	婆	夜	○
Duo	Ta	Qie	Duo	Ye	○	Duo	Di
哆	他	伽	多	夜	○	哆	地
Ye	Ta	○	O	Mi	Li	Dou	Po
夜	他	○	阿	彌	利	都	婆
Pi		O	Mi	Li	Duo		Xi
毗	○	阿	彌	利	哆	○	悉
Dan	Po	Pi		O	Mi	Li	Duo
耽	婆	毗	○	阿	彌	唎	哆
	Pi	Jia	Lan	Di		O	Mi
○	毗	迦	蘭	帝	○	阿	彌

Rebirth in Pure Land Dharani

Uprooting all Karmic Hindrances and Attaining Rebirth in the Pure Land Dharani

[Uprooting All Karmic Hindrances and Attaining Rebirth in the Pure Land Dharani is preserved in Sanskrit through Chinese transliteration. Traditionally dharanis are not translated. This dharani is recited following the chanting of the *Amitabha Sutra*.]

(repeat three times)

Li	Duo		Pi	Jia	Lan	Duo	
唎	哆	。	毗	迦	蘭	多	。
Qie	Mi	Ni		Qie	Qie	Na	
伽	彌	膩	。	伽	伽	那	。
Zhi	Duo	Jia	Li		Suo	Po	He
枳	多	迦	利	。	娑	婆	訶

(三稱)

Zan Fo Ji
讚 佛 偈

O	Mi	Tuo	Fo	Shen	Jin	Se	,
阿	彌	陀	佛	身	金	色	，
Xiang	Hao	Guang	Ming	Wu	Deng	Lun	.
相	好	光	明	無	等	倫	。
Bai	Hao	Wan	Zhuan	Wu	Xu	Mi	,
白	毫	宛	轉	五	須	彌	，
Gan	Mu	Cheng	Qing	Si	Da	Hai	.
紺	目	澄	清	四	大	海	。
Guang	Zhong	Hua	Fo	Wu	Shu	Yi	,
光	中	化	佛	無	數	億	，
Hua	Pu	Sa	Zhong	Yi	Wu	Bian	.
化	菩	薩	眾	亦	無	邊	。
Si	Shi	Ba	Yuan	Du	Zhong	Sheng	,
四	十	八	願	度	眾	生	，
Jiu	Pin	Xian	Ling	Deng	Bi	An	
九	品	咸	令	登	彼	岸	。

Praise to Amitabha Buddha

Amitabha Buddha's body is golden in hue;

His marks of excellence and brilliance are
incomparable.
His white tuft of hair curls like the five Mount
Sumerus;
His azure eyes are as clear as the four great
oceans.
His aura transforms into countless trillions of
Buddhas and
Manifests bodhisattvas without limit.

With his forty-eight vows he liberates all sentient
beings and
Enables all the nine ranks to reach the other
shore.

Nan	Mo	Xi	Fang	Ji	Le	Shi	Jie
南	無	西	方	極	樂	世	界
Da	Ci	Da	Bei	O	Mi	Tuo	Fo
大	慈	大	悲	阿	彌	陀	佛

Cheng Song Mi Tuo Sheng Hao
稱誦彌陀聖號

Nan	Mo	O	Mi	Tuo	Fo
南	無	阿	彌	陀	佛
O	Mi	Tuo	Fo		
阿	彌	陀	佛		

We take refuge in Amitabha Buddha of Great Kindness and Compassion in the Western Land of Ultimate Bliss.

Reciting Amitabha Buddha's Name

We take refuge in Amitabha Buddha.

Amitabha Buddha.

Bai Yuan
拜 願

Nan	Mo	O	Mi	Tuo	Fo
南	無	阿	彌	陀	佛

Nan	Mo	Guan	Shi	Yin	Pu	Sa
南	無	觀	世	音	菩	薩

Nan	Mo	Da	Shi	Zhi	Pu	Sa
南	無	大	勢	至	菩	薩

Nan	Mo	Qing	Jing	Da	Hai	Zhong	Pu	Sa
南	無	清	淨	大	海	眾	菩	薩

Taking Refuge in Amitabha Buddha and the Bodhisattvas

We take refuge in Amitabha Buddha.

We take refuge in Avalokitesvara Bodhisattva.

We take refuge in Mahasthamaprapta Bodhisattva.

We take refuge in the pure, ocean-like assembly of bodhisattvas.

San Gui Yi
三 皈 依

Zi Gui Yi Fo Dang Yuan Zhong Sheng
o 自 皈 依 佛，當 願 眾 生，

Ti Jie Da Dao Fa Wu Shang Xin
體 解 大 道，發 無 上 心。

Zi Gui Yi Fa Dang Yuan Zhong Sheng
o 自 皈 依 法，當 願 眾 生，

Shen Ru Jing Zang Zhi Hui Ru Hai
深 入 經 藏，智 慧 如 海。

Zi Gui Yi Seng Dang Yuan Zhong Sheng
o 自 皈 依 僧，當 願 眾 生，

Tong Li Da Zhong Yi Qie Wu Ai
統 理 大 眾，一 切 無 礙。

Triple Refuge

I take refuge in the Buddha, wishing that all sentient beings understand the Dharma and make the supreme vow.

I take refuge in the Dharma, wishing that all sentient beings study the sutras diligently and obtain an ocean of wisdom.

I take refuge in the Sangha, wishing that all sentient beings lead the masses in harmony without obstruction.

Xiang O Mi Tuo Fo Qi Yuan Wen
向 阿 彌 陀 佛 祈 願 文

Ci Be Wei Da De O Mi Tuo Fo
慈 悲 偉 大 的 阿 彌 陀 佛！

Wo Mei Tian Lai Dao Nin De Zuo Qian
我 每 天 來 到 您 的 座 前，

Yi Ji Wei Gong Jing Qian Cheng De Xin Qing
以 極 為 恭 敬 虔 誠 的 心 情，

Cheng Nian Nin De Sheng Hao
稱 念 您 的 聖 號，

Li Bai Nin De Jin Rong
禮 拜 您 的 金 容，

Nin De Bai Hao Guang Ming Zhao Liang Zheng Ge Yu Zhou
您 的 白 毫 光 明 照 亮 整 個 宇 宙，

A Prayer to Amitabha Buddha

Oh great, compassionate Amitabha Buddha!

Every day I come before you

In an extremely respectful and sincere state of mind,

To chant your name and to pay respect to your golden image;

The light from the fine, white hair emanating from the middle of your brow illuminates the whole universe,

Nin De Fa Yan You Ru Hai Shui Yi Yang Qing Che
您 的 法 眼 有 如 海 水 一 樣 清 澈。

Wo Men You Zhong Di Gan Xie Nin Zai Jiu Yuan Jie Qian
我 們 由 衷 地 感 謝 您 在 久 遠 劫 前，

Fa Si Shi Ba Yuan Jiu Du Wo Men
發 四 十 八 願 救 度 我 們。

Nin Yu Shi Jie Qian Yuan Man Fo Dao
您 於 十 劫 前 圓 滿 佛 道，

Zhuang Yan Le Ji Le Jing Tu
莊 嚴 了 極 樂 淨 土。

Nin Na Li
您 那 裡，

Qi Bao Chi Zhong Lian Hua Duo Duo
七 寶 池 中 蓮 華 朵 朵，

Ba Gong De Shui Rou Ruan Qing Liang
八 功 德 水 柔 軟 清 涼，

Hang Shu Lou Ge Jing Ran You Xu
行 樹 樓 閣 井 然 有 序，

Xiang Feng Shi Lai Shu Yue Zhong Xin
香 風 時 來 舒 悅 眾 心，

Your Dharma eyes are as crystal-clear as the ocean.
We extend our heartfelt thanks to you
For initiating the forty-eight vows to liberate us
many kalpas ago,
And for adorning the Pure Land of Ultimate Bliss,
Therefore attaining Buddhahood
More than ten kalpas ago.

Where you are,
Lotus flowers cluster in the ponds of seven treasures,
The water of the eight virtues is soft, pure, and cool,
Orderly lined trees and towers abound,
Frequent breezes soothe and please the mind,

Fan Yin Miao Yue Chu Chu Piao Dang
梵 音 妙 樂 處 處 飄 盪，

Qi Hua Yi Niao Xuan Yang Fo Fa
奇 花 異 鳥 宣 揚 佛 法，

Yi Shi Wu Que Sui Xin Suo Xian
衣 食 無 缺 隨 心 所 現，

Zhu Shang Shan Ren Ju Hui Yi Chu
諸 上 善 人 聚 會 一 處，

Mei Ri Qing Dan Gong Yang Zhu Fo
每 日 清 旦 供 養 諸 佛。

Nin Na Li
您 那 裡，

Guo Tu Mei You Huan Jing De Wu Ran
國 土，沒 有 環 境 的 污 染；

Jing Ji Mei You Cai Chan De Zhan You
經 濟，沒 有 財 產 的 佔 有；

Sheng Huo Mei You E Ren De Can Hai
生 活，沒 有 惡 人 的 殘 害；

Chu Zhong Mei You Ren Wo De Shi Fei
處 眾，沒 有 人 我 的 是 非；

The sound of the Dharma and wonderful music
float everywhere,
Exotic flowers and unusual birds preach the Dharma,
Abundant clothing and food appear as one's heart
wishes,
All excellent beings gather in one place,
And with each dawn, offerings are made to all
Buddhas.

Where you are,
In the Pure Land of Ultimate Bliss,
There is no environmental pollution;
In economics, there is no argument over property;
In life, there is no cruelty from evildoers;
In dealing with people, there is no gossip;

Jiao You Mei You Cai Yi De Wu Hui
交 遊，沒 有 猜 疑 的 誤 會；

Zheng Zhi Mei You Po Hai De Yuan Qu
政 治，沒 有 迫 害 的 冤 屈；

Jiao Tong Mei You Shi Gu De Fa Sheng
交 通，沒 有 事 故 的 發 生；

She Hui Mei You Jie Ji De Cha Bie
社 會，沒 有 階 級 的 差 別。

Ci Bei Wei Da De O Mi Tuo Fo
慈 悲 偉 大 的 阿 彌 陀 佛！

Wo Yao Xiang Nin Qing Su
我 要 向 您 傾 訴，

Zai Wo Men Zhe Ge Wu Zhuo E Shi Li
在 我 們 這 個 五 濁 惡 世 裡，

Ren Yu Ren Zhi Jian Er Yu Wo Zha
人 與 人 之 間 爾 虞 我 詐，

Guo Yu Guo Zhi Jian Fen Zheng Bu Xi
國 與 國 之 間 紛 爭 不 息，

Wo Men De You Ku Ru Da Hai Ban De Shen Chen
我 們 的 憂 苦 如 大 海 般 的 深 沉，

Wo Men De Fan Nao Xiang Man Cao Ban De Mian Yan
我 們 的 煩 惱 像 蔓 草 般 的 綿 延。

In one's circle of friends, there is no misunderstanding;
In politics, there is no persecution or injustice;
In transportation, there are no troublesome incidents;
In society, there is no distinction in class.

Oh great, compassionate Amitabha Buddha!
I would like to unburden myself to you:
In our Saha world of the evil period of five degenerations,
There is deception and fraud among people,
There are unceasing conflicts among countries.
Our suffering is as deep as the ocean,
Our worries spread like creeping weeds.

Ci Bei Wei Da De O Mi Tuo Fo
慈悲偉大的阿彌陀佛！

Qi Qiu Nin Yi Ci Shi She Shou Wo
祈求您以慈誓攝受我，

Yuan Wo Zai Meng Mei Zhi Ji
願我在夢寐之際，

Neng Gou Jian Dao Nin De Jin Shen
能夠見到您的金身，

Neng Gou You Li Nin De Jing Tu
能夠遊歷您的淨土，

Neng Gou De Dao Nin De Gan Lu Guan Ding
能夠得到您的甘露灌頂，

Neng Gou De Dao Nin De Guang Ming Chu Zhao
能夠得到您的光明觸照，

Rang Wo Xiao Chu Su Ye
讓我消除宿業，

Rang Wo Zeng Zhang Shan Gen
讓我增長善根，

Rang Wo Jian Shao Fan Nao
讓我減少煩惱，

Oh great, compassionate Amitabha Buddha!

I pray to you to receive me through
your vows of loving-kindness.

In my dreams: May I see your golden body;

May I travel to and experience your Pure Land; May I

obtain your blessing by the sprinkling of
your Dharma water;

May I receive the illumination and touch of
your light;

May I eliminate past karma;

May I increase the wholesome roots;

May I decrease afflictions;

Rang Wo Ti Sheng Yuan Li
讓 我 提 昇 願 力。

Qi Qiu Nin Yi Bei Xin Du Hua Wo
祈 求 您 以 悲 心 度 化 我，

Rang Wo Zai Shi Yuan Yi Liao Shi
讓 我 在 世 緣 已 了 時，

Neng Gou Yu Zhi Shi Zhi Shen Wu Bing Ku
能 夠 預 知 時 至，身 無 病 苦；

Neng Gou Xin Wu Dian Dao Zheng Nian Fen Ming
能 夠 心 無 顛 倒，正 念 分 明。

Qi Qiu Nin He Pu Sa Sheng Zhong
祈 求 您 和 菩 薩 聖 眾，

Shou Chi Jin Tai Fang Guang Jie Yin
手 持 金 台，放 光 接 引；

Rang Suo You Jian Wen De Ren
讓 所 有 見 聞 的 人；

Dou Neng Huan Xi Zan Tan Fa Pu Ti Xin
都 能 歡 喜 讚 歎，發 菩 提 心；

Dou Neng Wen Miao Fa Yin Huo Wu Sheng Ren
都 能 聞 妙 法 音，獲 無 生 忍；

May I enhance the effectiveness of my vow.

I pray to you to liberate me with your compassionate heart;

When my time in the world has ended,

May I know it beforehand,

And not suffer from physical illness;

May I have no mental delusions,

And have clear, right mindfulness.

I pray to you, and all bodhisattvas,

To hold the golden throne in your hands and

Allow its light to draw and guide me;

May all who see and hear of this be joyous and appreciative,

Initiate the bodhi mind, hear the wonderful sound of the Dharma,

Rang Wo Neng Gou De Dao Nin De Shou Ji
讓我能夠得到您的授記，

Cheng Yuan Zai Lai Hong Fa Li Sheng
乘願再來，弘法利生；

Yuan Suo You De Zhong Sheng
願所有的眾生，

Dou Neng Gou Tong Sheng Xi Fang Yong Bu Tui Zhuan
都能夠同生西方，永不退轉。

Ci Bei Wei Da De O Mi Tuo Fo
慈悲偉大的阿彌陀佛！

Qing Qiu Nin Jie Shou Wo Zhi Cheng De Qi Yuan
請求您接受我至誠的祈願！

Qing Qiu Nin Jie Shou Wo Zhi Cheng De Qi Yuan
請求您接受我至誠的祈願！

And attain "the patience of the non-arising of phenomena";

May I receive your prediction of Buddhahood,

And come back again with vows to propagate the Dharma and benefit all beings;

May all sentient beings be reborn in the Pure Land of the West, and never regress.

Oh great, compassionate Amitabha Buddha!

Please accept my sincerest prayer!

Please accept my sincerest prayer!

Hui Xiang Ji
回向偈

Yuan Sheng Xi Fang Jing Tu Zhong
願生西方淨土中，

Jiu Pin Lian Hua Wei Fu Mu
九品蓮花為父母。

Hua Kai Jian Fo Wu Wu Sheng
花開見佛悟無生，

Bu Tui Pu Sa Wei Ban Lu
不退菩薩為伴侶。

Dedication of Merit

May I be reborn in the Western Pure Land,

With lotus flowers of the nine ranks as parents;

When the flowers blossom, I shall see the Buddha
and awaken to the truth of non-arising,

With non-regressing bodhisattvas as
companions.

O Mi Tuo Fo Si Shi Ba Da Yuan
阿彌陀佛四十八大願

Guo Wu E Dao Yuan She Wo
1. 國無惡道願：「設我
De Fo Guo You Di Yu E Gui
得佛，國有地獄、餓鬼
Chu Sheng Zhe Bu Qu Zheng Jue
畜生者，不取正覺。」

Bu Geng E Dao Yuan She Wo
2. 不更惡道願：「設我
De Fo Guo Zhong Tian Ren Shou Zhong
得佛，國中天人壽終
Yi Hou Fu Geng San E Dao Zhe
以後，復更三惡道者，
Bu Qu Zheng Jue
不取正覺。」

The Forty-Eight Vows of Amitabha Buddha

[1] If I should attain Buddhahood, yet there would be hell beings, hungry ghosts, or animals in my land, may I not attain perfect enlightenment.

[2] If I should attain Buddhahood, yet humans and heavenly beings in my land would again be in the three lower realms after the end of their lives, may I not attain perfect enlightenment.

Shen Zhen Jin Se Yuan She Wo
3. 身真金色願：「設我

De Fo Guo Zhong Tian Ren Bu Xi
得佛，國中天人不悉

Zhen Jin Se Zhe Bu Qu Zheng Jue
真金色者，不取正覺

。」

Xing Se Xiang Tong Yuan She Wo
4. 形色相同願：「設我

De Fo Guo Zhong Tian Ren Xing Se
得佛，國中天人形色

Bu Tong You Hao Chou Zhe Bu Qu
不同，有好醜者，不取

Zheng Jue
正覺。」

Su Ming Zhi Tong Yuan She Wo
5. 宿命智通願：「設我

De Fo Guo Zhong Tian Ren Bu Shi
得佛：國中天人不識

Su Ming Xia Zhi Zhi Bai Qian Yi
宿命，下至知百千億

[3] If I should attain Buddhahood, yet humans and heavenly beings in my land would not all be the color of genuine gold, may I not attain perfect enlightenment.

[4] If I should attain Buddhahood, yet humans and heavenly beings in my land would differ in appearance and vary in beauty, may I not attain perfect enlightenment.

[5] If I should attain Buddhahood, yet humans and heavenly beings in my land would not all be aware of their past lives and know events of at least the past hundreds of thousands of millions

Na You Ta Zhu Jie Shi Zhe Bu
那 由 他 諸 劫 事 者，不

Qu Zheng Jue
取 正 覺。」

Tian Yan Pu Jian Yuan She Wo
6. 天 眼 普 見 願：「設 我

De Fo Guo Zhong Tian Ren Bu De
得 佛，國 中 天 人 不 得

Tian Yan Xia Zhi Jian Bai Qian Yi
天 眼，下 至 見 百 千 億

Na You Ta Zhu Fo Guo Zhe Bu
那 由 他 諸 佛 國 者，不

Qu Zheng Jue
取 正 覺。」

Tian Er Pu Wen Yuan She Wo
7. 天 耳 普 聞 願：「設 我

De Fo Guo Zhong Tian Ren Bu De
得 佛，國 中 天 人 不 得

Tian Er Xia Zhi Wen Bai Qian Yi
天 耳，下 至 聞 百 千 億

Na You Ta Zhu Fo Suo Shuo Bu
那 由 他 諸 佛 所 說，不

of *nayutas*[1] of *kalpas*, may I not attain perfect enlightenment.

[6] If I should attain Buddhahood, yet humans and heavenly beings in my land would not attain heavenly vision and see at least hundreds of thousands of millions of *nayutas* of Buddhas' lands, may I not attain perfect enlightenment.

[7] If I should attain Buddhahood, yet humans and heavenly beings in my land would not attain heavenly hearing and hear the teachings of at least hundreds of thousands of millions of

1. A large number unit. It is the twelfth number of successively larger numbers with each one ten times greater than the preceding one.

	Xi	Shou	Chi	Zhe	Bu	Qu	Zheng	Jue
	悉	受	持	者，	不	取	正	覺
	。」							
		Ta	Xin	Xi	Zhi	Yuan	She	Wo
8.		他	心	悉	知	願：「	設	我
	De	Fo	Guo	Zhong	Tian	Ren	Bu	De
	得	佛，	國	中	天	人	不	得
	Jian	Ta	Xin	Zhi	Xia	Zhi	Zhi	Bai
	見	他	心	智，	下	至	知	百
	Qian	Yi	Na	You	Ta	Zhu	Fo	Guo
	千	億	那	由	他	諸	佛	國
	Zhong	Zhong	Sheng	Xin	Nian	Zhe	Bu	Qu
	中	眾	生	心	念	者，	不	取
	Zheng	Jue						
	正	覺。」						
		Shen	Zu	Wu	Ai	Yuan	She	Wo
9.		神	足	無	礙	願：「	設	我
	De	Fo	Guo	Zhong	Tian	Ren	Bu	De
	得	佛，	國	中	天	人	不	得
	Shen	Zu	Yu	Yi	Nian	Qing	Xia	Zhi
	神	足，	於	一	念	頃，	下	至

nayutas of Buddhas, and they would not receive and uphold all of them, may I not attain perfect enlightenment.

[8] If I should attain Buddhahood, yet humans and heavenly beings in my land would not attain the wisdom of mind reading and know the minds and thoughts of sentient beings of at least hundreds of thousands of millions of *nayutas* of Buddhas' lands, may I not attain perfect enlightenment.

[9] If I should attain Buddhahood, yet humans and heavenly beings in my land would not attain supernatural abilities and travel beyond at least hundreds of thousands of millions of *nayutas* of

Bu Neng Chao Guo Bai Qian Yi Na
不 能 超 過 百 千 億 那

You Ta Zhu Fo Guo Zhe Bu Qu
由 他 諸 佛 國 者，不 取

Zheng Jue
正 覺。」

Bu Tan Ji Sheng Yuan She Wo
10. 不 貪 計 生 願：「設 我

De Fo Guo Zhong Tian Ren Ruo Qi
得 佛，國 中 天 人 若 起

Xiang Nian Tan Ji Shen Zhe Bu Qu
想 念 貪 計 身 者，不 取

Zheng Jue
正 覺。」

Zhu Ding Zheng Mie Yuan She Wo
11. 住 定 證 滅 願：「設 我

De Fo Guo Zhong Tian Ren Bu Zhu
得 佛，國 中 天 人 不 住

Ding Ju Bi Zhi Mie Du Zhe Bu
定 聚 必 至 滅 度 者，不

Qu Zheng Jue
取 正 覺。」

Buddhas' lands within one thought, may I not attain perfect enlightenment.

[10] If I should attain Buddhahood, yet humans and heavenly beings in my land would give rise to perceptions, thoughts, or greed toward their bodies, may I not attain perfect enlightenment.

[11] If I should attain Buddhahood, yet humans and heavenly beings in my land would not abide in meditative concentration toward enlightenment and definitely attain nirvana, may I not attain perfect enlightenment.

Guang Ming Wu Liang Yuan She Wo
12. 光明無量願：「設我
De Fo Guang Ming You Neng Xian Liang
得佛，光明有能限量，
Xia Zhi Bu Zhao Bai Qian Yi Na
下至不照百千億那
You Ta Zhu Fo Guo Zhe Bu Qu
由他諸佛國者，不取
Zheng Jue
正覺。」

Shou Ming Wu Liang Yuan She Wo
13. 壽命無量願：「設我
De Fo Shou Ming You Neng Xian Liang
得佛，壽命有能限量，
Xia Zhi Bai Qian Yi Na You Ta
下至百千億那由他
Jie Zhe Bu Qu Zheng Jue
劫者，不取正覺。」

Sheng Wen Wu Shu Yuan She Wo
14. 聲聞無數願：「設我
De Fo Guo Zhong Sheng Wen You Neng
得佛，國中聲聞有能

[12] If I should attain Buddhahood, yet my light would have a limit and not illuminate at least hundreds of thousands of millions of *nayutas* of Buddhas' lands, may I not attain perfect enlightenment·

[13] If I should attain Buddhahood, yet my lifespan would have a limit and not be at least hundreds of thousands of millions of *nayutas* of *kalpas*, may I not attain perfect enlightenment.

[14] If I should attain Buddhahood, yet the number of *sravakas* in my land could be counted, even if their number is known only after all the sentient

Ji Liang Nai Zhi San Qian Da Qian
計量，乃至三千大千

Shi Jie Zhong Sheng Xi Cheng Yuan Jue
世界眾生悉成緣覺，

Yu Bai Qian Jie Xi Gong Ji Jiao
於百千劫悉共計校，

Zhi Qi Shu Zhe Bu Qu Zheng Jue
知其數者，不取正覺

。」

Sui Yuan Xiu Duan Yuan She Wo
15. 隨願修短願：「設我

De Fo Guo Zhong Tian Ren Shou Ming
得佛，國中天人壽命，

Wu Neng Xian Liang Chu Qi Ben Yuan
無能限量，除其本願

Xiu Duan Zi Zai Ruo Bu Er Zhe
修短自在。若不爾者，

Bu Qu Zheng Jue
不取正覺。」

Bu Wen E Ming Yuan She Wo
16. 不聞惡名願：「設我

beings of a three thousandfold world systems would become *pratyekabuddhas*[2] and count together for hundreds of thousands of *kalpas*, may I not attain perfect enlightenment.

[15] If I should attain Buddhahood, the lifespan of humans and heavenly beings in my land would be infinite, except for those who shorten their lives at will because of their original vows. If this should not be the case, may I not attain perfect enlightenment.

2. One who is awakened through dependent originaion without having heard the teachings of a Buddha.

De Fo Guo Zhong Tian Ren Nai Zhi
得佛，國中天人，乃至

Wen You Bu Shan Ming Zhe Bu Qu
聞有不善名者，不取

Zheng Jue
正覺。」

Zhu Fo Cheng Tan Yuan She Wo
17. 諸佛稱嘆願：「設我

De Fo Shi Fang Shi Jie Wu Liang
得佛，十方世界無量

Zhu Fo Bu Xi Zi Jie Cheng Wo
諸佛，不悉咨嗟稱我

Ming Zhe Bu Qu Zheng Jue
名者，不取正覺。」

Shi Nian Bi Sheng Yuan She Wo
18. 十念必生願：「設我

De Fo Shi Fang Zhong Sheng Zhi Xin
得佛，十方眾生，至心

Xin Le Yu Sheng Wo Guo Nai Zhi
信樂，欲生我國，乃至

Shi Nian Ruo Bu Sheng Zhe Bu Qu
十念，若不生者，不取

[16] If I should attain Buddhahood, yet humans and heavenly beings in my land would even hear the name of any unwholesomeness, may I not attain perfect enlightenment.

[17] If I should attain Buddhahood, yet immeasurable Buddhas in the worlds of the ten directions would not all praise and proclaim my name, may I not attain perfect enlightenment.

[18] If I should attain Buddhahood, yet sentient beings of the ten directions who aspire to be reborn in my land with wholehearted faith and joy, even having just ten thoughts [of my name], would not be reborn there, may I not attain perfect

Zheng Jue Wei Chu Wu Ni Fei Bang
正覺。唯除五逆，誹謗

Zheng Fa
正法。」

Lin Zhong Jie Yin Yuan She Wo
19. 臨終接引願：「設我

De Fo Shi Fang Zhong Sheng Fa Pu
得佛，十方眾生，發菩

Ti Xin Xiu Zhu Gong De Zhi Xin
提心，修諸功德，至心

Fa Yuan Yu Sheng Wo Guo Lin Shou
發願，欲生我國。臨壽

Zhong Shi Jia Ling Bu Yu Da Zhong
終時，假令不與大眾

Wei Rao Xian Qi Ren Qian Zhe Bu
圍繞現其人前者，不

Qu Zheng Jue
取正覺。」

Yu Sheng Guo Sui Yuan She Wo
20. 欲生果遂願：「設我

De Fo Zhong Sheng Wen Wo Ming Hao
得佛，眾生聞我名號，

enlightenment. The only exceptions are those who have committed the five great violations and those who have slandered the right Dharma.

[19] If I should attain Buddhahood, sentient beings of the ten directions would generate the bodhi mind, cultivate various virtues, and wholeheartedly vow to be reborn in my land. If at the end of their lives, I would not appear before them, surrounded by a great assembly, may I not attain perfect enlightenment.

[20] If I should attain Buddhahood, yet sentient beings who hear my name, concentrate their thoughts continuously on my land, cultivate all

Xi Nian Wo Guo Zhi Zhong De Ben
繫念我國，植眾德本。

Zhi Xin Hui Xiang Yu Sheng Wo Guo
至心迴向，欲生我國。

Bu Guo Sui Zhe Bu Qu Zheng Jue
不果遂者，不取正覺

。」

San Shi Er Xiang Yuan She Wo
21\. 三十二相願：「設我

De Fo Guo Zhong Tian Ren Bu Xi
得佛，國中天人，不悉

Cheng Jiu San Shi Er Da Ren Xiang
成就三十二大人相

Zhe Bu Qu Zheng Jue
者，不取正覺。」

Yi Sheng Bu Chu Yuan She Wo
22\. 一生補處願：「設我

De Fo Ta Fang Fo Tu Zhu Pu
得佛，他方佛土諸菩

Sa Zhong Lai Sheng Wo Guo Jiu Jing
薩眾，來生我國，究竟

roots of virtue, and wholeheartedly dedicate the virtue toward their aspiration to be reborn in my land would not fulfill their wishes, may I not attain perfect enlightenment.

[21] If I should attain Buddhahood, yet humans and heavenly beings in my land would not all have fully accomplished the thirty-two marks of a great man, may I not attain perfect enlightenment.

[22] If I should attain Buddhahood, all the multitudes of bodhisattvas in lands of other directions who come to be reborn in my land would ultimately reach [the stage of] being only one rebirth

Bi	Zhi	Yi	Sheng	Bu	Chu	Chu	Qi
必	至	一	生	補	處。	除	其
Ben	Yuan	Zi	Zai	Suo	Hua	Wei	Zhong
本	願	自	在	所	化，	為	眾
Sheng	Gu	Pi	Hong	Shi	Kai	Ji	Lei
生	故，	披	弘	誓	鎧，	積	累
De	Ben	Du	Tuo	Yi	Qie	You	Zhu
德	本，	度	脫	一	切。	遊	諸
Fo	Guo	Xiu	Pu	Sa	Xing	Gong	Yang
佛	國，	修	菩	薩	行，	供	養
Shi	Fang	Zhu	Fo	Ru	Lai	Kai	Hua
十	方	諸	佛	如	來，	開	化
Heng	Sha	Wu	Liang	Zhong	Sheng	Shi	Li
恆	沙	無	量	眾	生，	使	立
Wu	Shang	Zheng	Zhen	Zhi	Dao	Chao	Chu
無	上	正	真	之	道。	超	出
Chang	Lun	Zhu	Di	Zhi	Xing	Xian	Qian
常	倫	諸	地	之	行，	現	前
Xiu	Xi	Pu	Xian	Zhi	De	Ruo	Bu
修	習	普	賢	之	德。	若	不
Er	Zhe	Bu	Qu	Zheng	Jue		
爾	者，	不	取	正	覺。」		

away from Buddhahood. The only exceptions are bodhisattvas who have made the original vows to freely transform themselves: For the sake of sentient beings, they don the armor of the great vows, accumulate roots of virtue, and bring liberation to all; they travel through all Buddhas' lands, cultivate the bodhisattva practices, honor all Buddhas, Tathagatas, of the ten directions with offerings, edify sentient beings as immeasurable as grains of sand in the Ganges River, and establish them in the unsurpassed, true Way; they go beyond the usual practices of the grounds of the bodhisattva path, and manifest and cultivate the virtues of Samantabhadra. If this should not be the case, may I not attain perfect enlightenment.

Gong Yang Zhu Fo Yuan She Wo
23. 供養諸佛願：「設我
De Fo Guo Zhong Pu Sa Cheng Fo
得佛，國中菩薩，承佛
Shen Li Gong Yang Zhu Fo Yi Shi
神力，供養諸佛。一食
Zhi Qing Bu Neng Pian Zhi Wu Liang
之頃，不能遍至無量
Wu Shu Yi Na You Ta Zhu Fo
無數億那由他諸佛
Guo Zhe Bu Qu Zheng Jue
國者，不取正覺。」

Gong Ju Sui Yi Yuan She Wo
24. 供具隨意願：「設我
De Fo Guo Zhong Pu Sa Zai Zhu
得佛，國中菩薩，在諸
Fo Qian Xian Qi De Ben Zhu Suo
佛前，現其德本。諸所
Qiu Yu Gong Yang Zhi Ju Ruo Bu
求欲供養之具，若不
Ru Yi Zhe Bu Qu Zheng Jue
如意者，不取正覺。」

[23] If I should attain Buddhahood, and bodhisattvas in my land would honor all Buddhas with offerings through the spiritual power of the Buddha, yet they could not travel throughout immeasurable, innumerable millions of *nayutas* of Buddhas' lands within the time of a meal, may I not attain perfect enlightenment.

[24] If I should attain Buddhahood, and bodhisattvas in my land would manifest their roots of virtue in front of all Buddhas and honor them with offerings of their choice, yet they could not fulfill their wishes, may I not attain perfect enlightenment.

Yan Shuo Miao Zhi Yuan She Wo

25. 演說妙智願：「設我

De Fo Guo Zhong Pu Sa Bu Neng

得佛，國中菩薩，不能

Yan Shuo Yi Qie Zhi Zhe Bu Qu

演說一切智者，不取

Zheng Jue

正覺。」

Na Luo Yan Shen Yuan She Wo

26. 那羅延身願：「設我

De Fo Guo Zhong Pu Sa Bu De

得佛，國中菩薩，不得

Jin Gang Na Luo Yan Shen Zhe Bu

金剛那羅延身者，不

Qu Zheng Jue

取正覺。」

Yi Qie Yan Jing Yuan She Wo

27. 一切嚴淨願：「設我

De Fo Guo Zhong Tian Ren Yi Qie

得佛，國中天人，一切

Wan Wu Yan Jing Guang Li Xing Se

萬物，嚴淨光麗，形色

[25] If I should attain Buddhahood, yet bodhisattvas in my land could not teach [the Dharma] with all wisdom, may I not attain perfect enlightenment.

[26] If I should attain Buddhahood, yet bodhisattvas in my land would not attain the diamond-like body of *Narayana*,[3] may I not attain perfect enlightenment.

[27] If I should attain Buddhahood, humans, heavenly beings, and all myriad things in my land would be adorned and pure, brilliant and

3. A powerful Hindu deity adopted into Buddhism as one of the Dharma protectors.

Te Shu Qiong Wei Ji Miao Wu Neng
特殊，窮微極妙，無能

Cheng Liang Qi Zhu Zhong Sheng Nai Zhi
稱量。其諸眾生乃至

Dai De Tian Yan You Neng Ming Liao
逮得天眼，有能明了

Bian Qi Ming Shu Zhe Bu Qu Zheng
辨其名數者，不取正

Jue
覺。」

Dao Shu Gao Xian Yuan She Wo
28. 道樹高顯願：「設我

De Fo Guo Zhong Pu Sa Nai Zhi
得佛，國中菩薩，乃至

Shao Gong De Zhe Bu Neng Zhi Jian
少功德者，不能知見

Qi Dao Chang Shu Wu Liang Guang Se
其道場樹，無量光色

Gao Si Bai Wan Li Zhe Bu Qu
高四百萬里者，不取

Zheng Jue
正覺。」

beautiful, their shapes and colors would be extraordinary, and their utterly exquisite and wonderful qualities would be unfathomable and beyond description. If sentient beings, even those who have attained heavenly vision, could clearly distinguish the names and numbers of the wonders of beings and things there, may I not attain perfect enlightenment.

[28] If I should attain Buddhahood, yet bodhisattvas in my land, even those with few measures of virtue, could not know and see the bodhi tree with its immeasurable light and colors, four million miles in height, may I not attain perfect enlightenment.

Song Jing De Hui Yuan She Wo
29. 誦經得慧願：「設我
De Fo Guo Zhong Pu Sa Ruo Shou
得佛，國中菩薩，若受
Du Jing Fa Feng Song Chi Shuo Er
讀經法，諷誦持說，而
Bu De Bian Cai Zhi Hui Zhe Bu
不得辯才智慧者，不
Qu Zheng Jue
取正覺。」

Hui Bian Wu Xian Yuan She Wo
30. 慧辯無限願：「設我
De Fo Guo Zhong Pu Sa Zhi Hui
得佛，國中菩薩，智慧
Bian Cai Ruo Ke Xian Liang Zhe Bu
辯才，若可限量者，不
Qu Zheng Jue
取正覺。」

Zhao Jian Shi Fang Yuan She Wo
31. 照見十方願：「設我
De Fo Guo Tu Qing Jing Jie Xi
得佛，國土清淨，皆悉

[29] If I should attain Buddhahood, yet bodhisattvas in my land would not attain eloquence and wisdom after having received, read, recited, upheld, and expounded on the teachings of sutras, may I not attain perfect enlightenment.

[30] If I should attain Buddhahood, yet the wisdom and eloquence of bodhisattvas in my land could have a limit, may I not attain perfect enlightenment.

[31] If I should attain Buddhahood, my land would be pure, completely reflecting all the immeasurable,

Zhao Jian Shi Fang Yi Qie Wu Liang
照見十方一切無量

Wu Shu Bu Ke Si Yi Zhu Fo
無數不可思議諸佛

Shi Jie You Ru Ming Jing Du Qi
世界，猶如明鏡；睹其

Mian Xiang Ruo Bu Er Zhe Bu Qu
面像，若不爾者，不取

Zheng Jue
正覺。」

Bao Xiang Miao Yan Yuan She Wo
32. 寶香妙嚴願：「設我

De Fo Zi Di Yi Shang Zhi Yu
得佛，自地以上，至於

Xu Kong Gong Dian Lou Guan Chi Liu
虛空，宮殿樓觀，池流

Hua Shu Guo Zhong Suo You Yi Qie
華樹，國中所有一切

Wan Wu Jie Yi Wu Liang Za Bao
萬物，皆以無量雜寶，

Bai Qian Zhong Xiang Er Gong He Cheng
百千種香，而共合成。

innumerable, inconceivable Buddhas' worlds of the ten directions, just like seeing the image of one's face in a clear mirror. If this should not be the case, may I not attain perfect enlightenment.

[32] If I should attain Buddhahood, from the ground up into the sky, the palaces, towers, ponds, streams, flowers, trees, and all the myriad things in my land would all be made of an immeasurable number of various jewels and hundreds of thousands of kinds of incense. Their adornments would be marvelously exquisite, surpassing those of humans and heavenly beings. Their fragrances

Yan Shi Qi Miao Chao Zhu Tian Ren
嚴 飾 奇 妙， 超 諸 天 人。

Qi Xiang Pu Xun Shi Fang Shi Jie
其 香 普 薰 十 方 世 界，

Pu Sa Wen Zhe Jie Xiu Fo Xing
菩 薩 聞 者， 皆 修 佛 行。

Ruo Bu Er Zhe Bu Qu Zheng Jue
若 不 爾 者， 不 取 正 覺。」

Meng Guang Rou Ruan Yuan She Wo
33\. 蒙 光 柔 軟 願：「設 我

De Fo Shi Fang Wu Liang Bu Ke
得 佛， 十 方 無 量 不 可

Si Yi Zhu Fo Shi Jie Zhong Sheng
思 議 諸 佛 世 界 眾 生

Zhi Lei Meng Wo Guang Ming Chu Qi
之 類， 蒙 我 光 明 觸 其

Ti Zhe Shen Xin Rou Ruan Chao Guo
體 者， 身 心 柔 軟， 超 過

Tian Ren Ruo Bu Er Zhe Bu Qu
天 人， 若 不 爾 者， 不 取

Zheng Jue
正 覺。」

would permeate throughout the worlds of the ten directions, and bodhisattvas who perceive them would all cultivate the Buddha Way. If this should not be the case, may I not attain perfect enlightenment.

[33] If I should attain Buddhahood, sentient beings in immeasurable, inconceivable Buddhas' worlds of the ten directions whose bodies are touched by my radiant light would become soft and pliant in their bodies and minds to a degree surpassing that of humans and heavenly beings. If this should not be the case, may I not attain perfect enlightenment.

Wen Ming De Ren Yuan She Wo
34. 聞 名 得 忍 願：「設 我

De Fo Shi Fang Wu Liang Bu Ke
得 佛，十 方 無 量 不 可

Si Yi Zhu Fo Shi Jie Zhong Sheng
思 議 諸 佛 世 界 眾 生

Zhi Lei Wen Wo Ming Zi Bu De
之 類，聞 我 名 字，不 得

Pu Sa Wu Sheng Fa Ren Zhu Shen
菩 薩 無 生 法 忍，諸 深

Zong Chi Zhe Bu Qu Zheng Jue
總 持 者，不 取 正 覺。」

Tuo Li Nü Shen Yuan She Wo
35. 脫 離 女 身 願：「設 我

De Fo Shi Fang Wu Liang Bu Ke
得 佛，十 方 無 量 不 可

Si Yi Zhu Fo Shi Jie Qi You
思 議 諸 佛 世 界，其 有

Nü Ren Wen Wo Ming Zi Huan Xi
女 人 聞 我 名 字，歡 喜

Xin Le Fa Pu Ti Xin Yan E
信 樂，發 菩 提 心，厭 惡

[34] If I should attain Buddhahood, yet sentient beings in immeasurable, inconceivable Buddhas' worlds of the ten directions who hear my name would not attain the bodhisattva's patience of the non-arising of phenomena and the profound dharanis, may I not attain perfect enlightenment.

[35] If I should attain Buddhahood, and there would be women in immeasurable, inconceivable Buddhas' worlds of the ten directions who hear my name, rejoice with faith, generate the bodhi mind, and are weary of being women, yet after the end of their lives they would again be reborn as women, may I not attain perfect enlightenment.

Nü Shen Shou Zhong Zhi Hou Fu Wei
女身，壽終之後，復為

Nü Xiang Zhe Bu Qu Zheng Jue
女像者，不取正覺。」

Chang Xing Fan Xing Yuan She Wo
36. 常行梵行願：「設我

De Fo She Fang Wu Liang Bu Ke
得佛，十方無量不可

Si Yi Zhu Fo Shi Jie Zhu Pu
思議諸佛世界，諸菩

Sa Zhong Wen Wo Ming Zi Shou Zhong
薩眾，聞我名字，壽終

Zhi Hou Chang Xiu Fan Xing Zhi Cheng
之後，常修梵行，至成

Fo Dao Ruo Bu Er Zhe Bu Qu
佛道。若不爾者，不取

Zheng Jue
正覺。」

Tian Ren Zhi Jing Yuan She Wo
37. 天人致敬願：「設我

De Fo Shi Fang Wu Liang Bu Ke
得佛，十方無量不可

[36] If I should attain Buddhahood, all the multitudes of bodhisattvas in immeasurable, inconceivable Buddhas' worlds of the ten directions who hear my name would, after the end of their lives, always live the pure life of celibacy until they attain Buddhahood. If this should not be the case, may I not attain perfect enlightenment.

[37] If I should attain Buddhahood, all humans and heavenly beings in immeasurable, inconceivable Buddhas' worlds of the ten directions who hear

Si Yi Zhu Fo Shi Jie Zhu Tian

思議諸佛世界，諸天

Ren Min Wen Wo Ming Zi Wu Ti

人民，聞我名字，五體

Tou Di Ji Shou Zuo Li Huan Xi

投地，稽首作禮，歡喜

Xin Le Xiu Pu Sa Xing Zhu Tian

信樂，修菩薩行。諸天

Shi Ren Mo Bu Zhi Jing Ruo Bu

世人，莫不致敬。若不

Er Zhe Bu Qu Zheng Jue

爾者，不取正覺。」

Yi Fu Sui Yuan She Wo De

38. 衣服隨願：「設我得

Fo Guo Zhong Tian Ren Yu De Yi

佛，國中天人，欲得衣

Fu Sui Nian Ji Zhi Ru Fo Suo

服，隨念即至。如佛所

Zan Ying Fa Miao Fu Zi Ran Zai

讚應法妙服，自然在

Shen Ruo You Cai Feng Dao Ran Huan

身。若有裁縫擣染浣

my name, pay homage to me with a full prostration to the ground, and cultivate the bodhisattva practices would be revered by all heavenly beings and humans in the world without exception. If this should not be the case, may I not attain perfect enlightenment.

[38] If I should attain Buddhahood, humans and heavenly beings in my land would obtain any clothing they wish for as soon as they think it. They would naturally be clad in wonderful garments, which are in accordance with the Dharma and praised by Buddhas. If there should be any sewing, dyeing, or washing [needed], may I not attain perfect enlightenment.

Zhuo Zhe Bu Qu Zheng Jue
濯者，不取正覺。」

Le Ru Lou Jin Yuan She Wo
39. 樂如漏盡願：「設我

De Fo Guo Zhong Tian Ren Suo Shou
得佛，國中天人所受

Kuai Le Bu Ru Lou Jin Bi Qiu
快樂，不如漏盡比丘

Zhe Bu Qu Zheng Jue
者，不取正覺。」

Shu Zhong Xian Cha Yuan She Wo
40. 樹中現剎願：「設我

De Fo Guo Zhong Pu Sa Sui Yi
得佛，國中菩薩，隨意

Yu Jian Shi Fang Wu Liang Yan Jing
欲見十方無量嚴淨

Fo Tu Ying Shi Ru Yuan Yu Bao
佛土，應時如願，於寶

Shu Zhong Jie Xi Zhao Jian You Ru
樹中，皆悉照見。猶如

Ming Jing Du Qi Mian Xiang Rou Bu
明鏡，睹其面像。若不

[39] If I should attain Buddhahood, yet humans and heavenly beings in my land would not enjoy happiness like that of a *bhiksu* who has eradicated his outflows, may I not attain perfect enlightenment.

[40] If I should attain Buddhahood, whenever bodhisattvas in my land wish to see the immeasurable number of pure, adorned Buddhas' lands of the ten directions, they would fulfill their wish right then and see all of them reflected in jeweled trees, just like seeing the image of one's face in a clear mirror. If this should not be the case, may I not attain perfect enlightenment.

Er Zhe Bu Qu Zheng Jue
爾 者， 不 取 正 覺。」

Zhu Gen Wu Que Yuan She Wo
41. 諸 根 無 缺 願：「設 我

De Fo Ta Fang Guo Tu Zhu Pu
得 佛， 他 方 國 土 諸 菩

Sa Zhong Wen Wo Ming Zi Zhi Yu
薩 眾， 聞 我 名 字， 至 於

De Fo Zhu Gen Que Lou Bu Ju
得 佛， 諸 根 缺 陋 不 具

Zu Zhe Bu Qu Zheng Jue
足 者， 不 取 正 覺。」

Qing Jing Jie Tuo Yuan She Wo
42. 清 淨 解 脫 願：「設 我

De Fo Ta Fang Guo Tu Zhu Pu
得 佛， 他 方 國 土 諸 菩

Sa Zhong Wen Wo Ming Zi Jie Xi
薩 眾， 聞 我 名 字， 皆 悉

Dai De Qing Jing Jie Tuo San Mei
逮 得 清 淨 解 脫 三 昧。

Zhu Shi San Mei Yi Fa Yi Qing
住 是 三 昧， 一 發 意 頃，

[41] If I should attain Buddhahood, yet all the multitudes of bodhisattvas in lands of other directions who hear my name would suffer any lack or imperfection in their faculties at any time before attaining Buddhahood, may I not attain perfect enlightenment.

[42] If I should attain Buddhahood, all the multitudes of bodhisattvas in lands of other directions who hear my name would fully attain the *samadhi*[4] of pure liberation. They would abide in this *samadhi*, and as soon as they think of honoring immeasurable, inconceivable Buddhas, World-Honored Ones, with offerings, they would

4. A state in which the mind is conentrated in a one pointed focus.

Gong Yang Wu Liang Bu Ke Si Yi
供養無量不可思議

Zhu Fo Shi Zun Er Bu Shi Ding
諸佛世尊，而不失定

Yi Ruo Bu Er Zhe Bu Qu Zheng
意。若不爾者，不取正

Jue
覺。」

Wen Ming De Fu Yuan She Wo
43. 聞名得福願：「設我

De Fo Ta Fang Guo Tu Zhu Pu
得佛，他方國土諸菩

Sa Zhong Wen Wo Ming Zi Shou Zhong
薩眾，聞我名字，壽終

Zhi Hou Sheng Zun Gui Jia Ruo Bu
之後，生尊貴家。若不

Er Zhe Bu Qu Zheng Jue
爾者，不取正覺。」

Xiu Xing Ju De Yuan She Wo
44. 修行具德願：「設我

De Fo Ta Fang Guo Tu Zhu Pu
得佛，他方國土諸菩

accomplish this within a thought without losing their state of concentration. If this should not be the case, may I not attain perfect enlightenment.

[43] If I should attain Buddhahood, all the multitudes of bodhisattvas in lands of other directions who hear my name would be reborn in noble families after the end of their lives. If this should not be the case, may I not attain perfect enlightenment.

[44] If I should attain Buddhahood, all the multitudes of bodhisattvas in lands of other directions who hear my name would be joyful and enthusiastic,

Sa Zhong Wen Wo Ming Zi Huan Xi
薩 眾，聞 我 名 字，歡 喜

Yong Yue Xiu Pu Sa Xing Ju Zu
踴 躍，修 菩 薩 行，具 足

De Ben Ruo Bu Er Zhe Bu Qu
德 本。若 不 爾 者，不 取

Zheng Jue
正 覺。」

Pu Deng San Mei Yuan She Wo
45. 普 等 三 昧 願：「設 我

De Fo Ta Fang Guo Tu Zhu Pu
得 佛，他 方 國 土 諸 菩

Sa Zhong Wen Wo Ming Zi Jie Xi
薩 眾，聞 我 名 字，皆 悉

Dai De Pu Deng San Mei Zhu Shi
逮 得 普 等 三 昧，住 是

San Mei Zhi Yu Cheng Fo Chang Jian
三 昧，至 於 成 佛，常 見

Wu Liang Bu Ke Si Yi Yi Qie
無 量 不 可 思 議 一 切

Zhu Fo Ruo Bu Er Zhe Bu Qu
諸 佛。若 不 爾 者，不 取

cultivate the bodhisattva practices, and be replete with roots of virtue. If this should not be the case, may I not attain perfect enlightenment.

[45] If I should attain Buddhahood, all the multitudes of bodhisattvas in lands of other directions who hear my name would fully attain the *samadhi* of universal equality. They would abide in this *samadhi* until they attain Buddhahood, and they would always see all the immeasurable, inconceivable Buddhas. If this should not be the case, may I not attain perfect enlightenment.

Zheng Jue
正覺。」

Sui Yuan Wen Fa Yuan She Wo
46. 隨願聞法願：「設我

De Fo Guo Zhong Pu Sa Sui Qi
得佛，國中菩薩，隨其

Zhi Yuan Suo Yu Wen Fa Zi Ran
志願所欲聞法，自然

De Wen Ruo Bu Er Zhe Bu Qu
得聞。若不爾者，不取

Zheng Jue
正覺。」

Wen Ming Bu Tui Yuan She Wo
47. 聞名不退願：「設我

De Fo Ta Fang Guo Tu Zhu Pu
得佛，他方國土諸菩

Sa Zhong Wen Wo Ming Zi Bu Ji
薩眾，聞我名字，不即

De Zhi Bu Tui Zhuan Zhe Bu Qu
得至不退轉者，不取

Zheng Jue
正覺。」

[46] If I should attain Buddhahood, bodhisattvas in my land would naturally hear the Dharma they wish for in accordance with their aspirations and vows. If this should not be the case, may I not attain perfect enlightenment.

[47] If I should attain Buddhahood, yet all the multitudes of bodhisattvas in lands of other directions who hear my name would not instantly reach [the stage of] not regressing, may I not attain perfect enlightenment.

De San Fa Ren Yuan She Wo
48. 得 三 法 忍 願：「設 我

De Fo Ta Fang Guo Tu Zhu Pu
得 佛，他 方 國 土 諸 菩

Sa Zhong Wen Wo Ming Zi Bu Ji
薩 眾，聞 我 名 字，不 即

De Zhi Di Yi Di Er Di San
得 至 第 一、第 二、第 三

Fa Ren Yu Zhu Fo Fa Bu Neng
法 忍，於 諸 佛 法 不 能

Ji De Bu Tui Zhuan Zhe Bu Qu
即 得 不 退 轉 者，不 取

Zheng Jue
正 覺。」

[48] If I should attain Buddhahood, yet all the multitudes of bodhisattvas in lands of other directions who hear my name would not instantly reach the first, second, and third [states of] Dharma patience and not instantly attain [the stage of] not regressing from the Dharma of all Buddhas, may I not attain perfect enlightenment.

Fo Guang Shan
International Translation Center

Fo Guang Shan International Translation Center is dedicated to translating and distributing quality translations of classical Buddhist texts as well as works by contemporary Buddhist teachers and scholars. We embrace Humanistic Buddhism, and promote Buddhist writing that is accessible, community-oriented, and relevant to daily life. On FGSITC.org you can browse all of our publications, read them online and even download them for FREE, as well as requesting printed copies for you or your organization.

Donors

3965 copies	三寶弟子
2000 copies	佛光山光明寺護法信眾
1500 copies	Jia Peir Wang & Yueh Chin Hsu Wang
833 copies	蔡月琴、Dennis Wang & Derek Wang
500 copies	Andy Kaoh
333 copies	San Diego Buddhist Association
300 copies	Chiu Chen Maher, Jesse Wu., Wen Jong Wu
250 copies	李紹傑
200 copies	佛光山三寶寺護法信眾、佛光山菩提寺護法信眾、關志明
166 copies	萬美之
150 copies	蔣紅梅
145 copies	林依細、林葉妹合家
133 copies	Joy Lee
125 copies	新馬寺(南馬協會)
100 copies	佛光山香雲寺、溫哥華佛光山、邁阿密佛光山、于昆萍、丘幗媚、江嵐、江濤、吳張彩雲、李喜馨、李葉道香、李麗蓉、周麗香、林美瑜、林美緻、林蔡寶珍、林寶貞、徐行簡、郭家駿、陳林江旭、陳林江凌、陳林英俤、陳林彬、黃尹駿、黃美金合家、

黃國明、葉雪英、蔡淑敏、蔣麗玲、鄭曉萍、劉宸廷、劉淑芹、劉鎧霆、劉馥瑜、賴昭明、賴益祥、賴益程、賴益賢、藤文、蘇國斌、蘇慧敏、Venerable Man Jung, Esther Man, Vic & Chu Wu

99 copies　蘭傳俊

85 copies　沈香雲

83 copies　趙資東、趙資盈

80 copies　許麗娟

75 copies　郭克非

65 copies　留婉婉、張樑溪

60 copies　吳明瑾

51 copies　余冠全

50 copies　人間佛教研究院、關島佛光山、刁傳忠、方林慈嬉合家、方登發合家、王克英、王克德、王禪娟、司徒渠、司徒關瑞華、何美寶、余鄺惠嫻、吳琴琴、杜育玲、沈娟娣、沈婕、李國雄、李琳、周錦蓮、林健華、林培淮、林參繞、林逸心、林蕙如、林麗玉、林巍、姚意敏合家、倪碧琳、徐少文、徐汋欣、郭明煌、郭展洲、郭展斌、郭敏慧、郭劉麗金、郭麗珊、陳和平、陳宛怡、陳美玲、陳美鳳、陳莉雯、陳森、陳嫩妹、陳碧儀、留許秀瓊、黃世英、黃瑜田、曾芊芊、曾敏、曾瓊鶯、黃于文、黃玉雪、黃麗明、黃寶寶、葉依仁合家、廖秀鈴、蔡冬梅、蔡曉燕、劉忠、劉錫鵬、戴光廷、戴嘉逸、謝午萍、謝樂眉、謝鎮濤、魏玉盆合家、羅桂專、Thi Nhu Suong Bui, Emma Chen, Stella Chen, Aiden Egger, Brian Egger, Lillian Egger, Sylvia Egger, Jonathan

Hsieh, Paula Hsieh, Yu-Chun Kuo, Cheng Chai Lee, Ha Lee, Jeffrey Lee, Thomas Lee, Wayyie Lee, Michelle Liu, Raymond Ng, Katia Tam, ELM Customs Brokerage Inc., KC Global Insurance Agency, Mountain Tea Co.

45 copies 蘇雅慧

40 copies 王葉秀蓮、黃彩瑩、劉佳欣

37 copies 施相如

35 copies 楊意玲、Ann Fornaro, David Grosvenor, Bruce Zhou

34 copies Anh Thuan Huynh Family, Hoa Buu Van Huynh Family, Nick Lee Family

33 copies 方克難、方鈺、江永林、江永煬、余健華合家、吳允民合家、李貞利、張淑貞

30 copies 于寶雲、朱美英、朱喬明、江盈滿、阮呂芳周、阮呂曼玉、吳劉綺雲、李玉嬋、李何雲、卓雅芬、周美惠、林景嵐、郭家、陳玉峰、陳柏廷、陳淑玲、馬真、連桂子、馮家賢、黃氏仙、葉治宏、劉又嘉、劉旭恒、鍾松杉、關許彥、關鷹、十方理財保險公司、Fen-Ing L. Chang, Casey Chau, Lemon Hien Family, Helen Leong, David S Lin, Raphael Lukov, Kelley Yao Wang

29 copies 李健新

27 copies 王謝盆、楊林碧

25 copies 永訓法師、永餘法師、有承法師、依煌法師、滿機法師、王大洋、王專治、王煊亭、王鈺棟、朱名譽、阮呂月嬌、何李成、吳玉枝、李卓華、李卓瑛、李明河、李譚淑冰、卓淑姬、林曉典、林靜珍、林耀、洪國華、洪譽芯、洪譽烝、徐翔、莊麗美、郭孟琪、陳文錫、陳泓叡、陳玲玲、陳家祥、陳愛儀、陳繼偉、陳繼堯、馬燕貞、高瑞玉、張世濱、張履安、張馨月、許少波、許梓豪、許梓熠、許貴婷、梁煥英、梁曉信、

梁曉峯、曾梁煥英、曾德鴻、曾德鴻、黃玉理、黃玲棽、黃紹安、蔡佩盈、蔡素蓮、蔡淑淑、鄭子昱、鄭文昱、鄭丹寧、鄭伊儒、鄭伯昱、鄭喜文、歐桂瑛、潘伯滄、潘沛揚、潘勝利、黎秀英、劉久男、劉王者鈺、劉怡君、劉恆宇、蕭曉倩、Yu-Hui Fu, Louvenia Ortega, Thi Hue Quach, Ranie Setiani, Anh Tram

23 copies 郭倚龍、郭瓊儀

21 copies 王美詩、姚金榮、陳美珠、梁民里道、Mei Ching Chen

20 copies 有道法師、妙新法師、妙齊法師、依宏法師、友田理惠、心煦、文磊、王樂翰、王歡歡、石翠玉、任風斌、邢益蓮、何秀媚、何金蘭、何美潔、何偉影、何張少蘭、余作舉、余夢婷、余愛芳、吳小虹、吳雁南、吳聖平合家、吳麗華、杜祖芳、杜堡惜、沈安東、沈伯益合家、沈依婷、沈時豪、沈繼榮、李秀梅、李美雲、李貞雲、李偉成、李榮燦、周文俊、周沈夏鳳、周凌霄、林玉英、林延美、林明珠、林潔英、林燕、林興國、俞慧婭、施美齡、柯玉琴合家、胡振強、夏宇、奚會暘、孫秀娟、孫偉銘、孫淑芝、孫源源、孫顯東、徐央君、莊李文貞、郭美岑、陳玉蕊、陳呈成、陳秀英、陳李玉雙合家、陳紅蓮、陳偉才、陳游言、陳福治、陳慧芝、高睿宏、高睿禧、張宇清、張延、張彥慶、張婍、張貴媚、張靜林、曹思蕾、曹維鵬、麥圓觀、梁沁淼、梁栢鴻、曾瑞康合家、游宗熙、馮嘉曦、黃小洪、黃玉卿、黃玉燕、黃玉麗、黃明泰、黃家璧、黃海棠、黃華娟、黃啟泰、黃淑珍、黃凱詩、黃婷筠、黃榮川、黃榮宗、黃漂西、黃漢林、黃漢德、黃鳳德、葉恩碩、葉粉妹、楊何金鳳、楊琨琳、路正國、蔡美鸞、蔡素芬、蔣曼如、趙浩誼、鄭金鳳、鄭婷之、鄭穎桐、歐世浩、歐宇娟、歐敏、潘安麗、劉迪生、劉冠邦、劉偉城、劉誠德、蕭萬居、蕭龍生、賴廷睿、賴映如、謝淑嬌、鍾月慶、鍾廷昭、鍾秀娜、鍾紹康、韓勇惠、羅天和、羅峯、羅慧芝、羅錦蘭、鐘倩儀、Logan Chan, Toshiko Chang, George Chen, Francis Grosvenor, Agnes Ho, Tinh Hoang, Tommy Hsu, Henry Lukov, Victor Lukov, Calvin Luu, Jasmine Nguyen, Thi Ng Oan Nguyen, Olivia Yi Ong, Brittany Sin

18 copies　姚莉莉

17 copies　覺安法師、古美香、古菊香、令文允、朱雲翠、邱燕玲、李敏、周子昂合家、林鷺明合家、施創才、莊芳齡、郭思遠、郭桐羽、高岳、張健、張鄧金葉、喬于修、喬宣時、喬偉良、程蔚賢、馮怡雯、黃佩淑、黃春燕、黃瑜如、楊淑真、雷光明、雷慧、廖良玉、蔡光洲、趙旭、劉江、劉菁華、劉傑、Alice Hsiao, Kam Huynh Family, Nghi Huynh Lee, Vinh C. Huynh Family, Thong Luu & Nga Huynh-Luu, Samuel Lee Family, Joey Liu, Ya-Wen Ru, Vivian Tsai, Nick Wang, Kevin Wu

16 copies　滿容法師、成孝先、朱倫、李嬌娜、林陳雲香、陳秀蓉、傅永棻、潘彥寧合家、霍永鉅、Kim Dang

15 copies　心慧法師、知圓法師、阮呂中、阮呂近藤直子、何麗溶、吳鈁、吳詩涵、吳詩琳、周一恕合家、周倩平、林仲山、陳吳血、張婉薇、張雲傑、許宗賢、董素楨、馮錦秀、楊子江、楊立琪、劉家君、劉家彤、劉振常、謝德貴、鍾秀瓊、譚冰、Brenda Huang, Elissa Liu, Sonia Liu, J.G. Custom Tile, Inc.

13 copies　周胤安、謝淑子

12 copies　王春玲、王紅玲、王群海、吳超、周佑容、周邁平、柳鳳祥、馬天祐、高張文妹、張娟、趙桂美、鄧建民合家、劉櫻雪、戴張麗真、譚維漢

11 copies　王美珍、余木英、余芳、李飛陽、周培垚、徐玉蘭、陳彥文、張東來、曾弘毅、曾金國

10 copies 心拙法師、心誠法師、心憑法師、永懺法師、如培法師、有住法師、有榮法師、妙迦法師、妙澄法師、妙鎮法師、妙鐘法師、知航法師、知貫法師、知理法師、知願法師、會宗法師、滿宜法師、慧浩法師、丁月華、丁玉書、刁偉汶、刁潔怡、于合龍、于靜雯、于靜霞、于馥瑋、友田芳美、文紹治、方冠南、方美美、方健華、方黎菁、方靜、王士祥、王介強、王月琴、王玉坪、王亦基、王如萍、王江弘、王芳蜜、王建華、王明涓、王郁湄、王柯旦、王洪麗華、王秋雲、王香粉、王柳、王珠嬌、王珮琪、王偉馨合家、王培湄、王惟雲、王淑珍、王淑玲、王雪彬、王普玉、王黃秀芼、王意媚、王煒章、王蔡秀慧、王嬌、王賽鈺、王麗兒、王麗湄、付綠珍、古芬妮、古慧亮、司徒汶珊、司徒俊德、司徒崇贊、司徒彩瓊、司徒麗燕、左漢權、田秀花、申幼珍、申競、伍瑞雲、如心燕、如世清、如芳靚、如意、如意偉、如意順、如鈺仁、如澤鎧、如薇薇、如鍾怡、朱英蘭、朱洪日、江可兒、江玉珠、江秀卿、江振德、江桂芬、江璿、阮呂蔓、阮呂艷、初芝涵、何美穎、何書明、何書鄉、何莉莉、何慧群、何曉記、余月華、余昭艷、吳小鳳、吳文職、吳永順、 吳玉惠、吳伯堂、吳孝松、吳孝桉、吳志強、吳邱街市、吳佩燊、吳佳敏、吳依仁、吳金諓、吳冠焱、吳崇輝、吳淑敏、吳菁娥、吳雪娜、吳善智、吳筱琴、吳慧雯、吳錦鑾、宋季安、宋恩平、宋恩宇、宋善萱、宋善儀、杜和明、杜美華、杜純、肖小華、邱全春、邱宗彬、邱家炳、邱偉山、邱偉斌、邱國樹、邱楨瑩、邱翠瑩、邱緻瑩、邱寶玉、邵馨慧、沈艾琳、呂佳玲、呂美瑛、呂時英、李少珠、李文升、李台元、李永強、李玉箴、李光平、李吳淨朗、李依鴻、李忠原、李昇彥、李是界、李美珍、李素珍、李祥龍合家、李張美盈、李淑江、李淑美、李淑禎、李森堆、李翔昇、李舜武、李雲鵬、李黃玉枝、李誠一、李誠輝、李漢榮、李瑤、李慧儀、李燕菲、李錦波、依珍珍、卓宜豐、周立德、周安之、周偉鴻、周曼之、周梅桂、周逸之、周景忠、周楊璇吟、周漪娜、周漪婷、周銘希、周慧貞、周潔芬、周麗葉、官天佑、官瑞齡、官慧珊、官慧琛、官錦堃、明加怡、明慧盈、明慧敏、范真堆、范翎、林大珍、林女、林少珍、林玉貞、林玉梅、林宇卓、林廷、林芮安、林尚志、林明妗、林明正、林郁婷、林采菱、林亭妍、林美珍、林純芳、林素、林素妃、林陳阿良、林陳淑真、林添丁、林逸良、林琳、林楚忠、林煒釗、林筠惠、林麗香、林寶勇、林顯勳、侯宗佑、侯建國、侯昆佑、姜寶霞、施貝雯、施淇雅、施萬雷、施燕珠、施麗瓊、柯門合家、柯炯炯、柯孫義、柯森子、段華康、洪及泉、洪文檀、洪浚涵、洪祥安、洪淑均、洪淑真、洪淑惠、洪勢津、洪楷驊、洪毓旋、洪澤安、相素俠、紀瓊珠、胡秀璇、胡淑嫻、胡智彬、胡慧珍、胡鏝鈺、倪嘉言、唐大平、唐杏玲、夏萱、奚羅拉、孫筱琍、孫筱雯、孫銘浩合家、孫黎斌、徐瑞梅、徐潔好、徐興維、徒陳碧麗、紋谷向凜、紋谷直孝、紋谷咲凜、翁雪媚、莊建峯、莊茗蕎、莊寅彩、莊登翔、莊傳成、華鳴、袁潔珍、袁曉宏、郭小芬、郭玉珍、郭建成、郭國賢、郭張美珍、郭敏敏、郭琳娜、郭舜蘭、郭瑜、郭麗雲、陳仁妙、陳文嶸、陳月華、陳仙領、陳正、陳玉燕、陳白薇、陳何潔珍、陳吳玉鳳、陳秀玲、陳秀媚、陳秀慧、陳秀麗、陳芳序、陳李素蓮合家、陳宓、陳居財、陳怡君、陳泓瑋、陳林芳琴、陳冠吾、陳品慈、陳奕全、陳姝蓉、陳思思、陳映璟、陳映融、陳柏軒、陳炳麒、陳珍珍、陳皇絜、陳盈戎、陳紅錦、陳美吟、陳美茜、陳美華、陳軍、陳軍英、陳玲玲、陳時儂、陳素梅、陳堃康、陳淑慧、陳清瀅、陳雪如、陳惠貞、陳琳娜、陳雅玲、陳順官、陳愛珍、陳愛蓮、陳煌明、陳群、陳詩昀、陳嘉嘉、陳榮照、陳漢婷、陳碧桃、陳肇根、陳慶麟、陳潔明、陳蕙蘭、陳銳、陳應賢、陳鏵琳、陳韻妮、陳麗珍、陳識因、陳寶治、陳鑑強、馬丁德彬、馬長環合家、馬素芳、馬麗娟、高郁鈞、高金好、高林絹、高國豪、高惠玲、高朝見、高嘉敏、高薇淳、連阿財、連黃秀英、留平敏、留芳芳、留港財、留榜石、留聯泰、陸正炯、陸秋薇、區汶揚、崔秀珠、崔許輕梅、康韶賓、張于震、張亦慧、張再齡、張佩霞、張味姝、張岩、張明華、張秉東、張珂珂、張紅、張偉森、張婕妤、張淑美、張進、張琥昌、張雲美、張愛蘭、張義揚、張聖煜、張寧凱、張德昌、張靜文、張靜倫、張靄蘭、曹承玲、曹涓賢、曹啟順、符朱滿香、符惟如、許再舜、許芝碩、許建評、許明亮、許敏慧、梁志華、梁志偉、梁志雄、梁秋霞、梁鈺銘、梁興榮、隆觀、傅桂香、單萍、彭月英、彭丹鳳、彭民祥合家、彭碧霞、曾乃祺、曾天財、曾田、曾欣儀、曾美子、曾珠佩、曾培基、曾瑋儀、曾慧梅、曾錦鈴、曾麗華、游琇玲、程小蓮、程淑梅、董秀芳、董秀珍、費琮熹、費慕葦、雲餘下、馮少芳、馮雪兒、馮曾玉梅、黃仁德、黃少玲、黃氏娟、黃世榮、黃印福、黃玉仁、黃玉如、黃汝銘、黃佛賜、黃吳炎珠、黃妙霖、黃秀琴、黃佩蘭、黃佳鑫、黃建和、黃建封、黃治青、黃英展、黃厚輯、黃洪波、黃原力、黃桂芳、黃桂馨、黃華仕、黃郭明珠、黃國寶、黃淑雲、黃淳郁、黃清泉、黃斯瑄、黃斯瑜、黃琦瑛、黃詠思、黃順嬌、黃傳軒、黃煜珍、黃群傑、黃詩萍、黃資甯、黃種銘、黃聰樑、黃瓊瑢、黃麗娜、黃麗娥、黃麗蓉、黃寶梅、黃寶雲、葉士傑、葉秀蓮、葉玫玉、葉振興、葉桂梅、葉國勝、葉康琳、葉傳茗、葉壽忠、楊少璐、楊方鈺、楊玉如、楊光前、楊杜丹、楊宗淇、楊宗傑、楊宗翰、楊宛禎、楊宜禎、楊承翰、楊美雲、楊重雄、楊家漢、楊海平、楊紹東、楊畹蘭、楊榮芳、楊碧煙、楊綿蘭、楊學玢、楊燕玲、溫智凱、溫麗蒽、裘錦章、解鴻軍、詹李舜音、詹曼鈴、詹麗珠、靳雲法、廖玉蓮、廖有財、廖亞梅、廖林妝、廖保鈿、廖晏妮、廖婕苓、廖潔玲、廖潔雅、熊迪、熊雅慧、熊楊艷、熊瑞陽、翟業英、蔡月卿、蔡永純、蔡如春、蔡廷傑、蔡邱富美、蔡阿鏵、蔡亞水、蔡幸春、蔡忠文、蔡胡紅素、蔡家林、蔡華瑢、蔡惠宣、蔡藍詩、蔡壁雲、蔡鵬、蔣佩君、蔣佩佩、蔣素明、蔣國華、趙丹羽、趙巧容、趙宜、趙忠法、趙智邦、趙慈蓮、趙瑋靖、鄧金城、鄧淑賢合家、鄧嘉源、鄧燕芳、鄧寶玲、鄭天實合家、鄭文琴、鄭月雲、鄭正美、鄭伯能、鄭秀雨、鄭秀麗、鄭佩珍、鄭建豐、鄭金城、鄭景行、鄭義順、鄭嘉源、鄭澤霖、鄭薇、鄭錦、歐柱彬、歐綺霞、潘允、潘岳鵬、潘偉成、潘廣涉、潘麗芳、談麗珍、黎陳淑儀、劉天民、劉月嬉、劉丹、劉秀珠、劉忠信、劉林美、劉炫志、劉桂芳、劉嫚弟、冀承忍、蕭如意、蕭怡欣、蕭雅翎、蕭楚強、蕭嘉霓、蕭曉英、薛國英、薛嵩雲、賴美旭、錢俊宏、錢學儉、駱浩、駱凱芊、駱慷、駱寶生、盧大衛、盧世添、盧世聰、盧迎迎、盧家浩、盧蓉、盧澤坤、盧澤星、戴和威、謝心覺、謝信玉、謝黃芬芳、謝黃祝子、謝賜傳、鍾秀群、鍾雅芮、韓冠倫、韓政霖、韓詠詩、魏然、簡文達、簡志達、簡秀桂、簡祥祐、簡楊麗霞、簡鳳儀、顏文雄、瀚淑芝、蘇日彥、蘇欣欣、蘇研雲、蘇瑋璐、蘇錦浪、蘇麗麗、譚國基、關文水、龐兆佳、龐迪華、羅林偉儀、羅桂芬、龔文評、龔來俐、龔超斌、龔超群、龔瓊珠、Venerable Miaowei, Jason Chau, Johnny Chau, Luong Chau, Argus Chen, Brian Chen,Christopher Chen, Cynthia Hsu Chen,Michelle Chen, Shang Ling Chen, Kuuvui Chew, Geoff Chine, Tiffiny Chine, Sheila Clemente Go, San Jung Gu, Nguyễn Ngọc Hằng, Alexander Huang, Kaivika Huang, Marianne Huang, Jack Johnson, James F. Johnston, Sri. J, Truman Kwok, Daniel Lee, Grace Lee, Marty Lee, Kenny Leung, Jin Li, Mei Li, Peter Li, Shing Li, Jessica Lin, Lawrence Lin, Leo Lin, Miranda Lin, Philip Lin, Linh, Ieng Liu, Jamie Liu, Justin Liu, Gia Bao Luu, Sabrina Ma, Meggan, Alexandee W Moy, Katharine F Moy, Gia Linh Nguyen, Quang Khai Nguyen, Quang Minh Nguyen, Emily Pan, Jarden Pan, Ngoc Mai Phan, Victoria Ponce, Gia Du Quach, My Quan Quach, Kimberly Sheu, Ken Tjia, Marcus M Tjia, Nicolas Ken Tjia, Enno Tonn, Helen Tran, John Tran, Helen Yii Ling Tsai, Jeanne Tsai, Phạm Tùng, Stanley Twanmoh, Nguyen Quang Vinh, Anh Vo, Anna Wang, Gloria Wong, Aric Wu, Alexander Jiaze Xia, Elena Meng Xia, Evan Jiahong Xia, HengYang Ye, Connie Yip, Alice Young, Carol Yi Yu Zhang, Jason Zhang, Liz Zhang, Rose Zhang

9 copies 劉亞華、蕭啓文

8 copies 吳永明、邵穎衡、陳彩娥、陳敏雄、梁鄧美嬋、葉明沛、葉城全、葉廖蜂仔、葉蜜施、葉應霖、葉聰衛、楊美鳳、楊美蓮、楊陳玲瑛、廖嘉敏、蔡潔輝七兄弟姐妹、蔣葉領香、鄧燁輝、劉彥妤、賴惟悅、Vivian Lau, Jason Lee, Michael Lee, Phyllis Lee, Richard Lee, Quek Ngoh Liam, Adam Moreno, Ernie Moreno, Karyn Moreno, Manuela Moreno, Siobhan Moreno, Carol Lee Tsai

7 copies 心眾法師、妙哲法師、依日法師、孔玲琪、王若鑫、王盛蕙、沈珍兒、呂霈儀、范瑞珍、唐小蓓、陳麗卿、鄭茜茜、Tina Quyen Chen, Mo Han Choy, Julie Thi Chu, Gregory Ross, Lan Fun Yan

6 copies 永印法師、依勤法師、知空法師、滿穆法師、王又曾、王令僑、王令興、王金世英、王威月、王婉茵、王敏慧、王楚涵、司徒美英、朱怡靜、

朱新根、江永業、李子瑄、李林美琴、李美玲、
李浩威、金侯玉玲、林風宏、林香玉、林慧玲、
林慧萍、林慧雯、紀江美津、胡傑、韋彥妃、
徐麗珍、郭秀珍、陳易亨、陳禹丞、高啟效、
張秀梅、張美玲、張淑鳳、許哲嘉、許哲維、
許意馨、彭錦渭、黃成中、黃威葳、黃麗富、
管邦翔、管翊里、蔡佩伻、潘玉均、潘錦如、
劉玉盈、劉佩珍、賴惠敏、謝朱愛慈、謝德群、
魏大程、蘇萬芊、蘇萬奕、Venerable Man Yee,
Celcine Harrison, Shy Tong Hong, Wen Jung Hsin, Stella Lee,
Ester Moreno, Kwan Kwan Quah, Pey Peng Ross, R N Seton,
Krista Swanson, Ivy Tan, Anabelle Tsai, Emilia Tsai, Gong Yang

5 copies

心均法師、心祥法師、心馗法師、心詠法師、
心寬法師、心應法師、心豐法師、地樑法師、
如住法師、如根法師、如輝法師、有度法師、
妙方法師、妙印法師、妙旭法師、妙貫法師、
妙境法師、妙覺法師、覺紹法師、丁麗紅、
方芳、方卓華、方莉莉、方富饒、方惠珠、方碧玉、
毛光裕、王乃欣、王又萱、王文炳、王水蓮、
王世良、王永威、王永健、王永毅、王玉治、
王志強、王沛、王沛儀、王建博、王怡儒、王東誠、
王林霞、王秋霞、王美英、王美玲、王美清、
王美鳳、王家朋、王悅謙、王啟豐、王淑穎、
王進財、王雪娟、王惠卿、王智仁、王葉烏奏、
王瑀、王筠、王熙貞、王翠綠、王德旺、王擎宇、
王靜娟、王鍇睿、王鏡燊、王麒瑋、王麗英、
王艷敏、古苓光、古瑞玲、史俊豪、史庭如、
史瑩瑩、左沛鑫、甘米月、甘瑞、白玉蓮、石宜順、
石維、伍永芳、伍立安、伍立淵、伍佑娜、伍佑峻、
伍李婉、伍長好、伍碧瑜、安慚、曲家林、曲艷梅、
朱宏淳、朱氏金鳳、朱根根、朱偉華、朱焄豪、
朱營春、朱韻茹、朱麗珍、朱麗雲、江碧霞、
江德健、江麗貞、阮秀妹、阮呂卉均、阮呂曾桃、
阮呂麗華、余炳成、余美蓮、余群、初玉坤、
初家齊、吳玉燕、吳秀玲、吳秀珠、吳秀鑾、

吳李寶儀、吳亞吟、吳承翰、吳俐儀、吳洵慧、吳美玲、吳胡瑞瓊、吳家坤、吳容政、吳振漢、吳敏慧、吳翊瑄、吳菊香、吳堯峰、吳景耀、吳潔貞、吳黎惠卿、吳盧麗雪、妙音、宋女、宋佳瑋、宋逸夫、杜金華、杜美卿、杜健豪、杜善啟、杜綺雯、杜聯雄、杜韻菊、杜寶薇、汪仁珊、狄仲傑、肖南、肖連生、邱和敬、邱致遠、邱綠槿、邵偉圖、邵啟康、邵啟熙、沈仁琪、沈金華、沈祥雲、沈毓鳳、呂夏蓮、呂惠愛、李子珊、李小雯、李日鵬、李王意、李立霖、李如珍、李妙珠、李妙嫦、李志偉、李秀珍、李秀蘭、李芹詩、李佩蓁、李佳、李佳蓉、李妹、李建强、李松欽、李欣、李育麗、李長明、李金碧、李金鴻、李林春霞、李品妤、李品萱、李洪活、李炳進、李美雲、李香玲、李宴林、李素珍、李素梅、李陳沛晴、李陳秋榮、李連豐、李彬、李晗、李梅芬、李淑珍、李淑儀、李萃、李斯煜、李裕偉、李黃秀芳、李夢兒、李楚洲、李碧榮、李銀珍、李諾恒、李諾政、李曜、李麗竹、李繼榮、李馨才、卓子豪、卓明美、卓南生、周加駿、周加麒、周芝楹、周杏芳、周南柏、周美兒、周香屏、周桂玉、周桂湘、周笑晨、周培蘭、周添壽、周清標、周寶兒、周鐘靈、屈穎、房金洲、房麗雲、明義軒、明義騰、明蘇秀媚、武麗芬、范鴻英、金周生、金國慶、金善笙、金欽中、金欽元、金欽文、易佳佳、林少妹、林月和、林沛熙、林秀芳、林秀春、林秀鳳、林秀霞、林佩華、林周勤妹、林和卿、林坤儀、林旻翰、林欣慧、林法妙、林的明、林英方、林俊儀、林俊興、林品慧、林恆進、林柏瑋、林美純、林晉安、林晏瑜、林書毅、林書頡、林真如、林陳月、林連娟、林祥生、林偉佳、林偉雯、林偉靈、林國棋、林彩雲、林清、林進興、林智衡、林湯梅玉、林羣翔、林毓卿、林碧霞、林慧程、林穎芝、林錦玲、林盧笑儂、林寶寶、林艷、林艷娉、俞偉康、姜美惠、姜賴月娥、施安娜、施吾萱、施吾樺、施宏澤、施洪嫦娥、施淑惠、施清迪、施惠馨、施養灝、施鵬鵬、柯志偉、柯志德、柯定、柯亮君、柯展葉、柯淑顏、柯敬、柯鍾霖、洪世總、洪秀華、洪育全、洪桔、洪清海、洪貴華、洪瑋懋、洪瑞淑、洪嘉欣、洪寧遠、洪德霖、洪慶安、洪靜怡、洪嚴連鳳、胡文軍、胡文清、胡世玉、胡欣媛、胡威、胡高級、胡詠麟、胡震強、胡錫位、胡寶譽、胡艷華、柳欽華、倪時耀、倪靜雯、唐玉琴、唐立麗、唐愛蓮、夏春偉、夏美珠、夏露嘉、孫文婷、孫采芸、孫梅雪、孫冀煒、徐乃育、徐秀芹、徐李慧蘭、徐菊卿、徐媛妹、徐惠芬、徐湛武、徐愷威、徐麗珠、秦正明、秦柯欣、翁平、翁依琳、翁琳珊、翁齊倩、莊李嫊英、莊明珍、莊淑瑩、莊葆珠、莊豪軒、莊鳳萍、莊麗玉、郭文文、郭水泉、郭平均、郭立其、郭佩珊、郭庭蕙、郭陳秀琴、郭貴娟、郭雲、郭黃雲葉、郭源壽、郭樂儀、陳乃瑜、陳大成、陳大容、陳大謀、陳允文、陳天賜、陳心怡、陳文機、陳月娥、陳世恩、陳世傑、陳世權、陳玉、陳由如、陳白市、陳延達、陳妍、陳志浩、陳志華、陳志強、陳志輝、陳秀花、陳秀英、陳秀國、陳秀蘭、陳芷昀、陳佳億、陳孟芝、陳建國、陳怡卉、陳英、陳英壽、陳非、陳金蓮、陳俊吉、陳俊霖、陳冠宇、陳咨君、陳彥宇、陳彥豪、陳彥熹、陳春安、陳昱翔、陳柏翰、陳炳堯、陳皇綸、陳美貞、陳美玲、陳美華、陳韋如、陳韋誠、陳省君、陳健何、陳家富、陳家貴、陳展龍、陳恩善、陳振寧、陳晁騏、陳桂華、陳珠錦、陳素美、陳素貞、陳華俊、陳華留、陳閃、陳烈國、陳偉国、陳張影娘、陳敏芝、陳淑惠、陳淑鑫、陳清泉、陳隆志、陳凱茵、陳凱菱、陳凱穎、陳鈞培、陳傳波、陳慈馨、陳瑞櫻、陳嘉雯、陳嘉豪、陳嘉駿、陳維文、陳適嫻、陳靚微、陳瑩如、陳曉明、陳樹英、陳興建、陳濬霏、陳聰輝、陳鍾、陳懷江、陳麗玲、陳麗珠、陳麗敏、陳麗賓、陳耀航、陶達榮、馬宏象、馬家豪、馬祺安、馬瑞娣、馬翠良、馬鳳鎂、高本傑、高為宜、高淑嫻、高惠芬、高德蘭、高麗香、連美麗、留俊傑、留婉茵、留煜棋、留薇倩、區振機、區敬文、區敬榮、區煒傑、區煒豪、崔音、常玟、常怡、張于震、張小玲、張小燕、張文燕、張吉祥、張君宏、張宏仁、張志偉、張芷欣、張芷晴、張言志、張良明、張坤鈴、張明長、張明賜、張明艷、張育瑄、張修誠、張思偉、張洪添、張美鳳、張展強、張悅琪、張書豪、張素華、張偉雙、張培鈴、張婕、張淑莉、張淑惠、張進福、張雪卿、張凱傑、張凱翔、張善明、張雅鈞、張順安、張瑋庭、張詩卉、張福慧、張嘉慶、張榮順、張瑪莉、張慧雯、張曉軒、張靜芝、張瓊華、張蘇明明、張耀輝、曹笑蓮、眭永傑、章詩迪、章詩雨、許人權、許力邦、許玉蕊、許如娥、許汶儀、許芳洋、許為本、許倩迪、許陳編、許淑芬、許惠兒、許琬琳、許竣安、許竣博、許貽成、許鈞棋、許雅岱、許歆田、許義明、許義麟、許鈺鼎、許嘉芸、許嘉洛、許嘉晴、許麗玉、閆瑜博、麥愛惜、梁子軒、梁少美、梁汝超、梁志群、梁肖英、梁定嫺、梁明華、梁家瑜、梁華、梁勝偉、梁惠蘭、梁肇禺、梁麗娥、傅子揚、傅桂梅、傅婉兒、彭小蓮、彭世恩、彭玉雙、彭宇堂、彭春玉、彭淑貞、彭聖傑、彭嘉正、彭鳳娟、彭德堂、曾少賢、曾徐美悅、曾素月、曾陳速鳳、曾梓軒、曾凱怡、曾凱恩、曾凱斌、曾凱慈、曾貴富、曾德金、曾瓊芬、曾瓊珠、游于萱、游子平、游卉庭、游吳金鍊、游原基、游敏鈴、游淑卿、游淨雯、游紹藤、游智光、游紫微、游慶霖、游靜子、湯文美、湯明珠、甯巧茹、甯巧慧、程紗、鄒宗祿、鄒隆平、鄒慶宜、鄒慶頡、鄔妙英、鄔頌明、鄔慧娟、馮一醬、馮安當、馮振強、馮桂培、馮荷晴、馮啟觀、馮淑真、馮韻倩、黃一葉、黃山界、黃文秀、黃月娥、黃月雲、黃水盛、黃芝飛、黃秀芳、黃秀英、黃亞媜、黃金順、黃亭瑜、黃俊佳、黃信嘉、黃思嘉、黃振仕、黃國良、黃國華、黃彩鳳、黃淑月、黃淑珍、黃淑華、黃進川、黃雪娥、黃貴勇、黃雅苓、黃雅雯、黃順娟、黃愛雪、黃愛勤、黃詩敏、黃鈺庭、黃嘉莉、黃婣、黃蓮香、黃慶香、黃潤慈、黃錦儀、黃燿陽、黃麗容、黃繼禎、黃耀良、黃齡慧、葉文英、葉秀瓊、葉春福、葉霖、葉耀文、楊冬梅、楊正君、楊正經、楊玉蘭、楊沛欣、楊偉雄、楊紹銘、楊雅堯、楊義、楊嘵初、楊蕙芳、楊曉華、楊曉暉、詹玉女、詹孟修、賈沁、賈濤、廖文昌、廖保馨、廖柚薇、廖炳煌、廖家榮、廖展億、廖境陽、廖慧君、廖樹昌、廖錦屏、管安群、蔡文傑、蔡劫誼、蔡宏慧、蔡良基、蔡良勝、蔡亞密、蔡佩芬、蔡其灌、蔡宜琳、蔡英楊、蔡金石、蔡桂芳、蔡桂林、蔡軒軒、蔡偉和、蔡偉揚、蔡國陽、蔡堅宜、蔡敏順、蔡進成、蔡進和、蔡博仁、蔡黃麗雲、蔡慈恩、蔡嘉祥、蔡嘉敏、蔡榮宣、蔡鄭靄文、蔡鳳嬌、蔡魯密、蔡壁玉、蔡麗真、蔡麗媚、蔣祖芬、蔣德恩、蔣嚴培珍、裴奇哲、趙幸美、趙俊宇、趙庭庭、趙庭懿、趙淑珍、趙愛蓮、趙興望、鄧志玲、鄧家俊、鄧家傑、鄧慧儀、鄧靜霞、鄭兆凱、鄭聿甯、鄭至中、鄭至光、鄭和泰、鄭宗仁、鄭武昌、鄭淑芳、鄭淑娟、鄭清賢、鄭戴善、鄭寶琴、鄭鑽紅、閻莉莉、齊名玨、齊輝、慧因、樊國妹、歐宏達、歐玟珊、歐梁淑卿、歐寶誼、滕小雯、潘金鳳、潘惠蘭、潘錦江、衛蔭雄、黎永幹、黎坤儀、黎俊瑋、黎勞次雲、黎愛蓮、劉邱善淑、劉明倫、劉林榮、劉美伶、劉美菊、劉敉君、劉桂香、劉善森、劉愛廷、劉愛清、劉詹碧銀、劉蕙芬、蕭少芬、蕭詠信、蕭詠智、蕭慧芳、蕭慧敏、蕭銳昆、薛宇辰、薛甯勻、薛順虹、薛榮滿、薛蕙馨、薛攀元、賴周敏華、賴顯駿、賴顯驤、鄺永旋、駱倩鳴、駱倩慧、駱惀、駱嘉昌、盧文玲、盧美好、盧婉儀、盧婕、盧惠燕、謝文郡、謝佩君、謝佳凌、謝宗佑、謝宗翰、謝定蘭、謝宛真、謝旻芯、謝旻栗、謝玟儀、謝品儀、謝啟泉、謝發鎮、謝業潤、謝嘉玲、謝榮庭、謝曙陽、謝蘊平、鍾政倫、鍾海霜、魏玉琳、魏立昌、魏郭婄、魏湘雲、魏業鴻、黏麗英、藍章華、藍黃雪貞、簡宏安、簡若霞、顏邑安、顏佳敏、顏宗富、顏建群、顏鈺芳、嚴文英、蘇子英、蘇仁生、蘇玉春、蘇玉雲、蘇汝謙、蘇美菁、蘇偉桃、蘇淑群、蘇葉蘭、蘇頌雅、蘇慧瓊、蘇鏡昌、譚玉玲、譚兆昌、譚廣業、關婉慧、關婉薇、關煒文、關禮賢、關艷萍、闞菊芳、羅志明、羅素虹、羅連卿、羅雪雲、羅朝明、羅朝華、羅朝偉、羅朝鴻、羅鳳娥、羅麗兒、羅懿琳、大光明紙廠公司、帝之寶商行、Alex 阮、Emma 阮、Jordon 阮、Linda Bai, Carl Bangloy, Christchin Bauman, Joseph Bauman, Rey Bhatti, Thomas Breetham, Jessica Breetham, Adam Li Chan, Carney Chan, Evan Chan, King Li Chan, Lauren Chan, Sivhour Sim Chan, Adaline Chen, Angela Chen, Thomas Chen, Tiffany Chen, Eugene Chen, Michael Cheng, Christopher J Ghirardi, Erwin C. Go, Jana Trisha T. Go, Jennifer T. Go, Leanne Hailey T. Go, Raisa Elise T. Go, Chuang Chun Han, Tuan Jung Hou, Karin Hsiao, Jinelle C. Huang, Jiselle C. Huang, Brian Johnson, Christine Kani, Anjali Kimball, Jeff Kimball, Julian Kimball, Vivian Kimball, Kris Kuneva, Kelly Kwak, Ada Lam, Bac Van Lam, Jackson Langat, Kim Langat, Pinky Langat, Philip Lee, Billy Li, Evan Li, Isabella Li, Nathan Li, Tony Li, Andrew Lin, John Lin, Wen Yeh Lin, Aileen Liu, Doris Liu, Ethan Liou, Fred Liu, Kien Anh Luu-Ninh, Shingya Ma, Constant Mok, Hien Thanh Nguyen, Thi Hoang Ninh, Chiao Ti Osier, Jazmine Osier, Maxwell Osier, Stephanie M. Qin, Jinky Alao Santizo, Wendy Shiao, Camilo Go Siong, Katherine Sun, Amy Thomason, Misherr Tseng, Kenny Ung, Leslie Tang Ung, Sukanya Vasna, Ratana Vasna, Vanida Vasna, Yuthaphong Vasna, Jenny Vuong, Gavin Wang, Holly Wang, Lily Wang, Ann M. Webster, John Wei, Lenny Wen, Wan-Na Wu, Jam Xia, Mimi Yip, Tommy Yip, Creighton Yung, Hayden Yung, Scott Yung, Harrison Zhao, Jacky Zou, Danny Zou, Consolacion A. Federer, BLIA Westminster Sub-Chapter

4 copies 妙度法師、于家莉、孔俊儀、王小雨、王糸吟、王沈碧琴、王怡茜、王明亮、王映之、王娘、王偲珊、王喬芸、朱道權、宋驊臻、杜達明、呂俊鵬、呂傑、呂曄、李文龍、李玉鳳、李秀蓮、李昆定、李明益、李冠廷、李思佳、李美麗、李鳳嫺、竺之偉、范阿春、范明田、范裴羢、

林子婷、林子彭、林正堃、林亞育、林彥志、
林昱彣、林雪雲、林源澧、林鳳吟、林澤根、
林瓊敏、施秀美、施亞洽、胡麗芬、宮下光永、
殷小燕、郭文明、郭愛竹、陳妹、陳品潔、
陳雪霞、張哲維、張哲綸、張啟亮、張嘉汶、
張德正、張慧因、梁基峻、萬少華、黃卓盡、
黃宣穎、黃春稻、黃晏珊、黃進益、黃理喬、
黃詩富、黃翠華、黃鳳元、黃增智、黃慧卿、
楊比得、楊婷婷、蔡陳椒、蔡麗香、趙偉、
鄭婧晗、鄭碧華、歐雁安、劉春華、劉淑金、
劉暘、蕭足妹、叢蓮香、蘇秀蘭、關建虹、
Candy, Aiden Hanyuan Chen, Tandy Li Chin Chen, Christine Lau, David Lau, Keung Lau, Michelle Lau, Qiaolu Lin, Jack Nicholls, Aida Palacio, Shon Pieters, Warren Taylor

3 copies

如眾法師、妙軒法師、妙會法師、妙遵法師、
知德法師、覺慈法師、文燕萍、王佩君、王忠仁、
王秋龍、王美璘、王徐秀鸞、王桂芳、王真、
王敏之、王甄甄、王筱霞、王鈺甯、王榮華、
王譯琪、田憶萍、朱明文、吳秀英、吳旻祐、
吳長馨、吳勇明、吳家俊、吳國發、吳崇誠、
吳詠靈、吳楊秀蓮、吳楚玢、吳嘉欣、吳漢偉、
吳銳堅、汪仁剛、汪仁豪、汪立生、邱瑞文、
邱鴻輝、李月琛、李可晴、李思彤、李素金、
李連利、李婕萍、李敏欣、李淑貞、李淑涓、
李嘉慧、李應務、李燿文、周宏達、周宛穎、
金華康、金瑞琴、林玉珍、林育如、施玉萍、
洪美沙、洪莞驊、孫嘉寧、徐月華、徐吟葉、
徐金德、徐鷺、莊阿春、莊珮霖、莫潔珍、袁中偉、
郭大維、郭亞二、郭炫琰、郭婷婷、郭發興、
陳文正、陳文傑、陳文婷、陳妙群、陳志韋、
陳和平、陳妹、陳明磬、陳怜君、陳奕誠、陳春莉、
陳秋玉、陳惟成、陳許淑珠、陳惠珍、陳惠玲、
陳瑛瑛、陳瑞康、陳嘉雯、陳謝玲娟、陳關生、
陳麗美、陳麗莉、陳覺龍、馬田明、高三川、
高方、高秦堂、高堂益、高張美雲、高嵐、陸世諺、

區健國、張志孝、張志強、張金珠、張美燕、張雪寧、張愛莉、張銀球、張豐城、梅本常、梅顯華、許亞明、許梨珠、許觀宏、陽麗娟、麥觀明、梁文輝、梁施月珍、梁淑芹、梁蔡德珍、彭建華、曾令英、曾美怡、曾潔心、曾馨慧、湯玉蘭、董玉儀、黃文譽、黃正忠、黃秀遠、黃冠霖、黃勁鋒、黃韋綾、楊石清、楊美媛、廖春娥、蔡坤全、蔡淑美、鄧泰健、鄧泰傑、鄧國燦、鄭志峰、鄭紅、鄭陽秋、鄭歆穎、鄭瑞玉、鄭增滎、鄭錦殿、潘俐伶、劉美華、劉貞珠、劉國星、劉龍駿、薛慶色、錢建萍、謝志文、謝佩岑、謝昭、謝偉添、簡振龍、龐孟嬌、羅文芳、雪梨光明分會、Ann 周、Jessica Chen, Amanda Cheng, Leah, Liu, Lili Liu, Lingwen Liu, Caidi Huang, George Morales, Norma Soonderam, Amy Thai, Brandon Thai, Brittney Thai, Bronson Thai, Jimmy Thai, Benjamin Tsai, Anderson Ung, Landon Ung, Nathan Ung, Patrick White, Zhen Zhao

2 copies 如宣法師、如啓法師、知榮法師、丁仁好、尤玲玲、王大威、王天恩、王天賜、王文基、王月英、王水仙、王存孝、王妙平、王昆鋒、王治堯、王若雁、王亭文、王信智、王秋生、王秋南、王秋星、王桉睿、王雪燕、王達志、王馭廷、王源滿、王煒興、王詩翎、王慧、王輝煌、王曉海、甘麗珍、石千宗、石庭禎、石晏榕、石浩廷、石馥甄、朱梓冰、江元新、江美霖、江慶章、邢意容、何妹、余錦茵、吳尹瀞、吳四妹、吳余瑩、吳坤瑩、吳忠武、吳金傳、吳修水、吳政諭、吳珍玲、吳家潮、吳振鑫、吳海莉、吳連伍、吳淑真、吳傑、吳尊文、吳貽桂、吳道川、吳德群、吳德環、吳龍山、吳麗君、吳麗莉、杜式才、杜欣欣、杜珊珊、汪子恆、汪怡君、汪品宥、汪品蓁、汪書賢、汪境育、邱美蒔、邱美璇、邱麗幸、邱麗瓊、邱麗蘇、呂思漫、李月華、李延澤、李秀英、李秀葉、李秀鳳、李佳蒙、李美萱、李美靜、李徐葉、李國卿、李惠玲、李瑞屏、李福、李僖明、周英利、周英奇、周紅姑、周美心、周路佳、周滿、周麗真、周寶山、苟莉、范水乾、范召羽、范光武、范光燕、范志成、范邱竹英、范沈玉美、范妹、范瑞珠、范德淵、范寶珠、金善瑛、林安曦、林秀明、林秀筠、林秀麗、林佳慧、林育正、林美華、林添龍、林進添、林森聰、林慧怡、侯秀燕、姚梓峰、姚梓順、施正南、施至鴻、施珊珊、施研安、施梓桓、施清樹、施雅萍、施滎舜、施慶璋、施學開、柯志建、柯玲玲、柯貴美順、柯貴麗意、洪秀嫌、胡月娥、胡志祥、胡博雅、胡磊、唐明廉、夏藝方、孫秀蕙、孫英玄、殷雅黎、莊名英、莊淑認、莊銘勝、郭大佳、郭芊伶、郭克棋、郭秀瓊、郭昀晴、郭林子、郭美珍、郭泰延、郭泰良、郭浚軒、郭祥興、郭嘉晉、陳天勳、陳木川、陳王秀治、陳冬菊、陳巧敏、陳玉春、陳玉飛、陳吉德、陳杏嬌、陳杏靜、陳佩華、陳卓永、陳亭樺、陳秋月、陳偉良、陳惜月、陳梓瑩、陳淑蓮、陳裕來、陳雅梅、陳慈旻、陳慈欣、陳煒童、陳筱珍、陳潔英、陳潤卿、陳鎮江、陳懷宇、馬逸婷、馬祺智、高素蘭、陸星予、陸星寧、陸盈蓁、陸益欽、張仁莉、張天訓、張文述、張包璵璠、張玉清、張志潔、張秋月、張美智、張美鳳、張美燕、張晉傑、張淑梅、張甜甜、曹恩郡、曹晏郡、梅理德、梅道、符國銹、符傳旻、符傳殿、許秀琴、許紅桔、許美珍、許曉君、梁小杏、梁君豪、梁晉誠、梁善棋、梁達智、彭玉霞、曾尹澍、曾尹璿、曾永成、曾麗娟、鄔佳娜、雲羿華、黃子榮、黃子睿、黃友福、黃王遜花、黃石華、黃兆崧、黃兆萱、黃秀雲、黃芸媚、黃宜妹、黃雨藤、黃金德、黃則、黃奕旺、黃彥豪、黃春旺、黃柏雄、黃恩庭、黃振成、黃振藩、黃桂華、黃素穎、黃華、黃梓夏、黃涵妤、黃智依、黃渝雯、黃琬珊、黃瑞琴、黃詩友、黃嘉慧、黃慧明、黃澤林、黃麗華、黃麗螢、葉玟君、葉素珊、楊尚志、楊松麗、楊若菁、楊梅、楊盛標、楊盛樟、楊麗雅、廖子瀅、廖宏紳、廖幸丰、廖葱、廖聰棟、蔡仁碹、蔡岳科、蔡俊傑、蔡科佳、蔡淑儀、蔡麗娜、蔡麗詩、趙玉蘭、鄧有強、鄧淑明、鄧淑儀、鄭世傑、鄭卓、鄭珊玲、鄭致遠、鄭凰偉、鄭凱元、鄭歆潔、鄭歆儒、歐柏杉、歐雪歡、歐凱庭、潘棟材、黎振良、黎敦海、黎詩音、劉玉静、劉玫岑、劉葦、劉福嬌、劉輝、劉麗玲、劉麗娟、蕭敬行、蕭翠女、賴致弘、酈家鳳、盧秀芳、戴黃秀芬、戴業俊、謝宗憲、謝彩玉、謝菲、謝瑩慧、鍾美珍、鍾瑞珍、簡妙圭、簡陳素香、顏劍琴、蘇國珍、蘇葉珠、蘇葉慶、蘇碧珊、譚兆亨、譚拾、譚凱云、羅淑英、鐘淑賢、Nick 周、Nicole 梁、Ingagit, Karina, Ridwan, Tet Phin Bong, Cheryl Ann Brown, Stephanie Yang Ling Chang, Jason Chen, Ronald Chen, Selena Chen, Caroline

Chou, Geoff N Coleman, Margaret Coleman, Choi Jin Cong, Jun Fui Cong, Li Na Cong,Brian Dai, Scott Dai, Jenny Doo, David Fraser, Johnathan Fraser, Susy Fraser, Thi Mai Ha, Betty Rusmiaty Halim, Alysha Haverkos, Beatriz Haverkos, Edna Haverkos, Jacob Haverkos, Samuel Haverkos, Stephen Haverkos, Jason Huynh, Jeanne Huynh, Jimmy Huynh, Khui Lan Kon, Karen Lee, Alyssa Li, Ellie Li, Kayden Li, Jimmy Chit Liang Liao, Po Lian Liu, Elsie Lo, Jenny Lo, Jacob Luong, Jaden Luong, David Ma, Janet Ma, Kieu Ma, Sandy Ma, Jose Y. Mateo, Robert Sandjaja Pangestu, Cameron Smith, Isabella Sun, Chen Hong Tao, Frank Tran, Justin Tran, Phuong Tran, Quang Tran, Sukhum Vasna, Amelia Yau, Ethan Yang, Stephen Yang, Connie Young, David Young, Whitney Young

1 copy

心由法師、如悅法師、有容法師、妙昱法師、知旭法師、知屏法師、知敏法師、知善法師、知廣法師、知徹法師、一止、丁莉麗、文近容、文麗娜第一個孩子、方景群、王八月娜、王小旻、王存佐、王安琪、王秀萍、王建忠、王明海、王思穎、王荏萱、王倩文、王海生、王涵妮、王清保、王博軒、王榮、王滿雲、王艷芬、丘東英、古君全、甘吳秋桂、甘佩儒、甘柏輝、甘拾光、伍時浩、伍國輝、伍媚倫、伍葉真如、吕红霞、安然、朱炳衡、朱嘉立、朱錦鳳、江水蓮、江白屏、江敏凌、江義麟、阮鳳娥、何佩佳、何佩珊、何明先、何品誼、何奕燕、何宥嫺、何陳春、何鴻清、佘家文、佘盛華、余佩美、余奕平、余奕欣、余睦佳、余鳳絲、吳小雲、吳文蘭、吳王月娥、吳永騰、吳羽庭、吳佩珊、吳佩瑾、吳孟武、吳孟瑾、吳宛芸、吳明良、吳松發、吳松聲、吳長霖、吳林槐、吳俊安、吳俐萱、吳俐璇、吳俐諭、吳保昌、吳柏宏、吳健三、吳寄、吳章耀、吳曾婉珍、吳琪琛、吳琴妹、吳楊麗茹、吳經華、吳趙愛花、吳黎明、吳競之、宋氏孝、宋曉茜、杜少珊、杜少音、杜少娟、杜少華、杜少梅、杜玉梅、杜式輝、杜沁頤、杜俞岑、杜美施、杜桂先、杜敬、杜福智、肖虹、邱永來、邱阿對、邱旺廷、邱泓諺、邱郁婷、邱品瑄、邱彥儒、邱振忠、邱瑞敏、邱廖春、邱馨慧、邱齡慶、邱顯智、阿山、沈其偉、沈怡萱、沈麗鳳、呂永康、呂桂、李仁傑、李仁智、李允安、李文健、李平守、李佑智、李妍枝、李杏菊、李杜麗香、李沛卓、李秀霞、李迎盈、李亞東、李佩珊、李定維、李建明、李承翰、李昆定、李明芬、李明揚、李明徹、李明輝、李明耀、李欣芝、李育薰、李金生、李金憲、李紅舞、李美蓮、李洛延、李家成、李浩玲、李笑瑛、李素玲、李偉俊、李婉瑋、李婕、李淑芬、李盛弘、李傑昇、李惠研、李斯福、李道益、李傳明、李慎梅、李瑜芳、李瑜蕙、李維仁、李維駿、李鳳娥、李潤有、李錦珊、李錦淵、李麗娜、亞倫莎南、周巨茗、周玉葉、周宜澄、周牲有、周美玲、周康寧、周敏飛、周淑敏、周菁筠、周愉純、周愉絜、周瓊瑚、周寶華、周艷玲、孟晨西、所琳、招泳平、招翠潔、招翠燕、招翠瓊、招潤威、招潤聯、招霞、武亞飛、武昕曈、武珮倫、武益倫、范小煒、范基權、范慶軍、金瓊蘭、易世奇、易明正、易思如、易珈如、易倩如、易偉權、林子桓、林子暘、林天榮、林天德、林文華、林月容、林再華、林志英、林志駿、林芯慈、林良珠、林宜霆、林承毅、林明慧、林明灣、林茂森、林金遂、林金鎣、林俊雄、林勇如、林威誌、林秋夫、林恩德、林恩賜、林珮鈺、林偉權、林國煌、林敏春、林敏雄、林淑霞、林許險、林雪金、林惠英、林雅雯、林楠順、林楠濠、林瑞枝、林資展、林稜凱、林鳳珠、林德能、林翰邦、林錦華、林靜雯、林瓊英、林蘭芳、林鷺飛、侯宇晴、侯昫宇、侯昱承、侯逸強、侯楷忻、侯漢延、姜千家、姜光祐、姜鳳英、姜瑩瑩、姜穎容、施珵濬、施雪娥、施逸柔、施議煌、施議煒、柯銀美、洪民、洪長成、洪祚裕、洪連珠、洪進利、洪渝珮、洪瑜靖、胡以寬、胡民耀、胡志英、胡秀霞、胡宗鏗、胡峻、胡華鋒、胡凱茵、韋協祥、韋林雪蓉、韋惠英、倪麗芳、孫凱琳、孫銘彤、孫銘謙、孫錦江、徐丁麗君、徐金蘭、徐崇倫、徐萱珉、徐煒智、徐榮松、徐滿成、徐顥、敖葉銀、柴春香、殷海春、殷曉珠、殷曉輝、殷曉蕾、秦明鳳、翁石州、翁宗傑、翁宜寧、翁柳英、翁淑真、耿君儀、莊采彤、莊富凱、莊渭璜、莊貴長、莊慧琪、莊臻全、莫少康、莫金蓮、莫金蘭、莫昶滔、莫麗秋、莫麗玲、莫麗娟、莫麗珠、莫麗嫦、華羽、袁國靜、郭世宗、郭卉芝、郭四妹、郭冠萱、郭洪榕、郭珮甄、郭帶堅、郭帶勤、郭富田、郭穎怡、郭簡粉、郭蘭英、陳允斌、陳友禮、陳少棋、陳文章、陳文雄、陳月見、陳世良、陳世昌、陳世釗、陳世達、陳永上、陳玉清、陳玉歌、陳石金、陳兆萍、陳余枝、陳君威、陳含笑、陳沚輿、陳秀、陳秀蘭、陳佩君、陳佩珊、陳佩惠、陳佳鑫、陳季安、陳宗保、陳建光、陳怡伶、陳昌福、陳明智、陳欣儀、陳玟如、陳玟欣、陳玟萍、陳秉孝、陳英傑、陳金順、陳亭因、陳亭而、陳彥亘、陳彥任、陳彥蓉、陳彥霖、陳思宇、陳映廷、陳映汝、陳映鐸、陳柏言、陳洪秋裡、陳洪碧蓮、陳炳宇、陳炳松、陳盈任、陳羿豪、陳羿銘、陳衍菘、陳亮競、陳家慶、陳恩娣、陳莉蓁、陳益視、陳崎曜、陳淑泙、陳淑貞、陳清萬、陳清龍、陳逸釗、陳富隆、陳琮葳、陳琮曜、陳葳、陳覃詩儀、陳愛貞、陳棰、陳瑋翔、陳筱薇、陳聖文、陳詩媖、陳頌霖、陳靖天、陳靖文、陳廖釵、陳彰記、陳漢偉、陳蔡玉里、陳慶惠、陳儒行、陳錦蓮、陳壐文、陳顗安、陳麗娜、陳麗香、陳顯松、馬芝蘭、馬志雄、馬逸帆、高漢揚、高漢儀、高漢鋒、高麗瓊、陸正江、陸秋玲、陸國英、區日陞、區泳姍、區晉熙、區桂芬、區詠鋒、區慶東、區寶慶、崔小玲、崔廣興、張仁和、張元豪、張六妹、張可欣、張玉鳳、張同興、張芝美、張芝滔、張芝齊、張君竹、張宏齊、張芮甄、張邑齊、張坤榮、張旻熙、張育誠、張彥錦、張美玲、張恩柔、張偉然、張淑芬、張清華、張傲凡、張剩勇、張敬聰、張開第、張開鈺、張順財、張新運、張楨楹、張源然、張群英、張聖賢、張廣然、張影玲、張學正、張鍾菊妹、張麗珠、曹米榜、曹吳貴美、曹芸禎、曹育正、曹育生、曹桂忠、曹桂貞、曹啟洲、曹燕霞、章素函、許可敏、許沛晴、許亞儀、許侑芯、許和益、許和榮、許明月、許思南、許恬蜜、許恬靜、許炳欽、許祐溱、許家和、許家榮、許真真、許涵淨、許淑音、許湘玲、許貴鶯、許楷傑、許遠定、許漢龍、麥國森、麥煥彩、梁丕仁、梁永健、梁卓昇、梁啟邦、梁基峻、梁婧琳、梁智堅、梁智熹、梁鈺生、梁潔玲、梁翠玲、梁麗清、梁艷玲、傅娟娟、傅家祥、傅懋璿、彭文強、彭文菁、彭偉文、彭偉紅、彭偉玲、彭偉斌、彭禮謙、彭耀生、曾美玉、曾香妹、曾雪梅、曾理、湯有榮、湯俊賢、董菁、覃秀玲、覃詩冰、辜世華、辜陳玉葉、鄒永康、鄒宜瑩、鄒皓瑋、鄒瑄琳、鄔佩珍、馮三妹、馮永思、馮連、馮蓮英、馮德元、黃士娟、黃子軒、黃小玲、黃世昭、黃正江、黃玉華、黃玉煜、黃圳銘、黃宇蓁、黃芳億、黃芷晴、黃招娣、黃明清、黃明豪、黃秉和、黃金鸞、黃冠霖、黃奕凱、黃奕誠、黃宣輔、黃柏健、黃柏霖、黃炳川、黃哲閣、黃家鳳、黃莉茵、黃國輝、黃培華、黃敏瑞、黃梽渭、黃淑娟、黃淑琴、黃博宇、黃惠萍、黃裕仁、黃順明、黃順麟、黃義倫、黃義凱、黃鈺婷、黃頌稀、黃榴先、黃賜棋、黃錦堅、黃賽英、黃麗蓉、黃寶鳳、黃櫻嬌、黃瓔珞、葉文連、葉世慶、葉世權、葉好凡、葉杏娣、葉秀玲、葉佩麗、葉建均、葉欣宇、葉長良、葉長枝、葉保蕙、葉冠均、葉珊儀、葉美、葉家豪、葉婉嫻、葉張玉綿、葉梅英、葉清壽、葉雅苓、葉雲錦、葉愛仙、葉群、葉嬌、葉麗雲、葉顥頤、楊士青、楊永進、楊如茵、楊杏英、楊秀英、楊宗長、楊承軒、楊承霈、楊修祺、楊恩妮、楊恩昕、楊恩慈、楊啟祖、楊淇偉、楊敦和、楊朝欽、楊森閔、楊詠儀、楊貴媛、楊雅棠、楊瑞和、楊慧琳、楊麗燕、楚光華、褚豔陽、詹力憲、詹于綜、詹文覺、詹汝嬌、詹浩傑、詹旋傑、詹詠婷、詹詠晴、詹達娥、廖玉廖、廖芳佑、廖松英、廖秉桓、廖秉婕、廖茂俊、廖珠君、廖得權、廖湧鈞、廖異晨、廖福南、廖翠麗、廖慧燕、廖滄蒼、廖靜萱、蔡文芳、蔡伊琳、蔡志雄、蔡秀彩、蔡林銓、蔡淑貞、蔡雅惠、蔡瑞摘、蔡瑞雯、蔡瑞銘、蔡瑞瑩、蔡群雄、蔡燕妮、蔡錫榮、蔣大理、蔣得匀、蔣得文、趙翠華、趙鋒翔、趙鋒榮、趙燕媛、鄧杜麗芬、鄧秀娥、鄧淑明、鄧楚芬、鄧壽諾、鄭九根、鄭尤翔、鄭月市、鄭世澤、鄭卉鳳、鄭亦真、鄭伊倪、鄭名珊、鄭汝笑、鄭聿均、鄭羽宸、鄭志偉、鄭忻語、鄭沁鈴、鄭沁鎂、鄭秀娟、鄭佳玉、鄭周秋妹、鄭孟軒、鄭炳輝、鄭韋建、鄭國樑、鄭張卿、鄭進益、鄭朝仁、鄭朝元、鄭游嫌、鄭紫燕、鄭詠兒、鄭慈仁、鄭慈惠、鄭詩穎、鄭赬、鄭鉦國、鄭嘉萱、鄭誌鵬、鄭磊萍、鄭燕葵、鄭錦裕、鄭龍你、歐陽秀德、潘汝珍、潘金真、潘惟梅、黎思敏、黎偉雄、黎國富、黎嘉敏、黎賽玲、劉太造、劉少玉、劉伶伶、劉見屏、劉侍瑛、劉欣、劉秉鈞、劉俊亨、劉俊甫、劉健華、劉陳桂妹、劉琇瑩、劉雅斌、劉瑞超、劉榕、劉樂凡、劉樂惟、劉燕好、劉耀智、蕭欣華、蕭富安、蕭慧鈞、蕭瓊鴛、薛由泉、薛由煌、薛昌清、薛明珠、薛來勇、薛美鳳、賴怡如、賴笑棠、賴進娣、賴齡艷、錢珮芸、駱麗芳、盧麗花、戴明榮、戴甜妹、謝正平、謝玉霞、謝仲顯、謝明諭、謝敏瑩、謝菊娥、謝達超、謝詩敏、謝嘉鳳、鍾玉珍、鍾林祥、鍾愛玲、韓陸慧、韓雪梅、韓瓊菊、魏好恩、魏彤思、魏秀英、藍習鎮、簡王金玉、簡柏賢、簡嬌、闕山頭、闕壯裕、闕抒安、闕抒恩、闕河彬、闕河堯、闕睿慈、闕睿儀、闕蔡文英、闕慧瑜、闕慧瑩、顏月英、顏金盆、嚴文昌、嚴敏禎、嚴凱彤、蘇仁信、蘇建中、蘇美心、蘇容瑾、蘇傳凱、蘇傳齡、蘇會婷、蘇鵬、譚敬澤、關燕萍、羅雲、羅煥華、羅煥鈴、龔志強、Amelia 王、Bastian, Chikara, Kenji, Lucky, Owen, Sofia, Hang An, Phuong Vy An, Feng Feng Cai, Amanda Chang, KeLan Chen, YingXiang Chen, Philip Cheung, Ellis Chiu, Gloria Chiu, Lim Chou, Dora Chung, Van Diep, Johnathan Fang, Kenneth Hardy, LiQiong Huang, Amanda Hui, Derek Hui, Jennifer Hui, Kitty Hui, Margaret Yen Chu Huang, Helen Can Huynh, Anth Jim, Theresa Jim, Kathy Jim, Tippy Kieth, Kim Chi Le, Clara S Lee, Ronald W Lee, Stephanie K Lee, Gloria Leung, Peter Leong, Frank Mu Hsien Liao, Jason Lowe, My Chau Ly, Nathan Ly, Trung Ly, Kenny Ly, Henry Manh, Kevin Manh, Jose Maria, Heng Gie Ng, Heng Lee Ng, Hui Xuan Ng, Don Nghiem, Quan Nghiem, Vu Manh Nguyen, Pauline Nguyen, Alexander Mukardi Pangestu, Angeline Pangestu, Melissa Pangestu, Michelle Pangestu, Giovanni Papa, Pham The Quyen, Tu Chau Quan, YaMei Shao, Raymend Jeff Sia, Monika Stefanescu, Caroline Tang, Marie Tang, Ang Li Thai, Albert Tran, Andrew Tran, Austin Tran, Benjamin Tran, Kelvin Tran, Pham Tran Mai Trinh, Benson Tsai, Tiffany Tsai, Rong Tsui, Natalie Tsui, Warren Tsui, Sasitha Tuntrakul, Tran Thi Thanh Van, Chalisa Vasna, Kanita Vasna, Pavee Vasna, Ratachai Vasna, Sasithorn Vasna, Phong Vi, Chih Chou Wang, Emily Wang, Lien Ly Wang,Kathy Wei, Ken Wei, Matthew Wei, Annie Wu Yip, Edward Yip, Hui Zhang,
A & M ewelry, Best Jewelry.

Thank you to all who donated to support the
printing and distribution of this booklet